KT-452-513

Debrett's

QUEEN ELIZABETH
THE QUEEN MOTHER

Her Majesty Queen Elizabeth the Queen Mother on the occasion of her ninetieth birthday.

Debrett's
QUEEN ELIZABETH THE QUEEN MOTHER

Valerie Garner

HEADLINE

Dedication
For Jennie and Joanna

First published in 1990
by Webb & Bower (Publishers) Limited
in association with Debrett's Peerage Limited

This edition published
by HEADLINE BOOK PUBLISHING
under licence from Webb & Bower (Publishers) Limited

10 9 8 7 6 5 4 3 2 1

Designed by Sue Stainton
Picture Research by Anne-Marie Ehrlich

British Library Cataloguing in Publication Data

Garner, Valerie
Debretts Queen Elizabeth the Queen Mother
1.Elizabeth, Queen, consort of George VI, King of Great Britain 2.Queens - Great Britain - Biography
I.Title
941'.084'092

ISBN 0 7472 2329 7

Printed and bound in Great Britain by
Butler and Tanner Ltd, Frome and London

HEADLINE BOOK PUBLISHING
A division of Hodder Headline PLC
338 Euston Road
London NW1 3BH

CONTENTS

Epsom Derby, June 1986.

Garter Ceremony, Windsor, June 1988

Sandringham Flower Show, July 1987.

'Though God hath raised
me high,
yet this I count the glory
of my crown:
that I have reigned with
your loves.'

QUEEN ELIZABETH I

Quoted at the Queen Mother's eightieth birthday Thanksgiving Service at St Paul's Cathedral by the Archbishop of Canterbury.

INTRODUCTION

SPANNING THE CENTURY

Elizabeth R

Lady Elizabeth Bowes Lyon aged twenty-three.

INTRODUCTION

SPANNING THE CENTURY

QUEEN Victoria's pessimistic forecast, echoed by her son Edward VII in the following reign, was that the British monarchy would not survive beyond the 1930s. This gloomy prediction might have been all too accurate if future monarchs had not had a saviour waiting in the wings; a child of the new century, born on 4 August 1990: the future Queen Elizabeth, the Queen Mother.

She, more than anyone, assured the stability of the monarchy as it entered the last decade of the twentieth century and she celebrated her ninetieth birthday. Her courage, resolution and the subtle magic she wove into public relations, had sustained and strengthened the Royal Family since the spring day in April 1923 when she became part of it.

Queen Victoria had always discouraged her family from smiling in public. She wished them to look solemn and worthy – even in family photographs – and it had become part of royal protocol ever since. But on her wedding day Lady Elizabeth Bowes Lyon's effervescent happiness was so irrepressible that newspapers called her 'The Smiling Duchess'. Churchill was to write, years later, when that famous smile became a national inspiration during the Second World War, that 'many an aching heart found solace' because of her cheerful stoicism. It was only a small change in a royal public appearance. But it was a

Queen Elizabeth the Queen Mother with the Red Arrows at RAF Scampton.

A royal bride. Elizabeth, still a commoner, leaves her Bruton Street home on 26 April 1923. For her return journey with her husband the new Duchess was escorted by the Household Cavelary

momentous one – the first of many the new Duchess introduced to the hitherto stolid and colourless reign of George V and Queen Mary.

As the first commoner bride of a royal prince in 250 years, Lady Elizabeth, youngest daughter of the Earl and Countess of Strathmore and Kinghorne, brought into the family 'a lively and refreshing spirit', according to her brother-in-law, the Prince of Wales – later King Edward VIII, then Duke of Windsor.

She wed Prince Albert (known as 'Bertie' within the family circle) the Duke of York, second son of the King and Queen, in Westminster Abbey where fourteen years later they would, most unexpectedly, be crowned King and Queen.

As Consort, Queen Elizabeth carried the refashioning of the Royal Family's public image a stage further – metaphorically drawing back the curtains and throwing open the windows to let in, not only daylight, but fresh air and sunshine too. Walter Bagehot, the Victorian historian, who laid down the definitive role of constitutional monarchy might have called it 'the march of improvement'. But only so much daylight was allowed to filter through to an outside world increasingly interested in the new family in the Palace. Even as a comparatively young woman, Queen Elizabeth was shrewd enough to note Bagehot's most famous edict on the monarchy: 'Its mystery is its life. We must not let in daylight upon magic', he counselled.

It was a lesson her mother-in-law Queen Mary, a perceptive authority on royalty, had always stressed and the new Queen managed to achieve a brilliant compromise. The King would maintain, as Dermot Morrah put it, 'a certain degree of aloofness'. But by his side would be a warm-hearted, charismatic Queen and two endearing Princesses, making an unbeatable combination as 'the family firm' – so dubbed by the King when they became established.

It was just what was needed after the trauma of Edward VIII's abdication in order to marry American divorcee Mrs Wallis Simpson, which had left the Crown somewhat lustreless, if not tarnished. As the then Governor-General of Canada, Lord Tweedsmuir (the author John Buchan) observed when she made, with the King, the first of many triumphant visits to Canada in 1939: 'Queen Elizabeth has a perfect genius for the right kind of publicity'. This flair for public relations coincided most happily with the fact that Queen Elizabeth's views on life tended to mirror those of 'the dear public', as she called her world-wide admirers. She stood for decency, home-making, hard work combined with plenty of fun and laughter with, almost certainly, 'a small drinky-poo' as she put it, at the end of the day.

On the threshold of history: a portrait of a young woman who became wife to and mother of a sovereign.

'Us four' . . . 'the family firm', so dubbed by George VI.

Here she is photographed with four of her grandchildren: the Prince of Wales; Prince Edward; the Princess Royal and the Duke of York.

Adolf Hitler was rightly wary of her charm, believing it made a significant contribution to Britain's war effort. 'The most dangerous woman in Europe', he called her – a title which much amused the King and Queen.

There was much laughter in all the Queen Mother's homes – Clarence House, Royal Lodge, Birkhall and the Castle of Mey. She enjoyed a near risqué joke and had her own brand of piquant humour from which no one was immune.

Respect for the sanctity of the crowned and annointed sovereign could sometimes include a little gentle teasing. Once when the Queen and the Queen Mother were lunching together at Clarence House, the younger woman decided, most unusually for her, to have another glass of wine. 'Is that wise?' said her mother, her eyes twinkling as she enjoyed her own joke. 'You know you have to reign all afternoon'. On another occasion, at Balmoral, the Queen found that the keys of the log cabin where they planned to have a picnic had been mislaid. 'But darling', said the Queen Mother, throwing her arms up, just a little, in one of her typical gestures, 'I thought all you had to say was "Open Sesame!" '

Despite the teasing – strictly within the family circle – Queen Elizabeth the Queen Mother was the sole remaining

living link with the founder of the present dynasty, Queen Victoria, and still maintained some of the standards of an earlier royal age. She was, after all, born a Victorian and tutored in protocol by that undoubted matriarch, her mother-in-law Queen Mary with whom she always got on famously.

Maintaining and enhancing the 'mystique' of the monarchy, if indeed such a thing existed as the century drew to a close, has been a policy the Queen Mother had always advocated and her husband and daughter followed. Sensitive to public opinion she learnt over nearly seven decades of playing a leading role that, however social fashions may change, the British like, and probably expect, the Royal Family to be different and to take their place above the traditional tiers of society. It helps if they appear human too, a seemingly impossible balancing act the Queen Mother performed impeccably ever since she became a public figure.

As the House of Windsor relaxed the rules on divorce and separations where they apply in unhappy royal marriages, the matriarch of the family had grown more flexible in her attitude. A relative whose marriage had broken down said the Queen Mother initially told her firmly: 'You must grit your teeth and try harder'. But 'after two years when we really had tried and failed, she was very sweet and understanding'.

There is no reason to suppose the Queen Mother did not say exactly the same to her daughter Princess Margaret and granddaughter the Princess Royal and her brothers when their marriages foundered. Perhaps over the years she came to see that a royal relationship is just as fallible as any other.

Although she lived most of her life in a blaze of publicity, the Queen Mother herself never, incredibly, put one of her tiny, size three and a half feet out of line. It was an achievement her two former granddaughters-in-law (the late Princess of Wales and the Duchess of York) might well have envied. This imperturbable professionalism could even be daunting to younger royals because the standards she set were so high. When they came to her, as they often did, distressed because of media criticism, the Queen Mother said more than once, with a trace of bitterness alien to her: 'We [the Royal Family] are not supposed to be human'.

She knew all the problems that can beset a member of the Royal Family because she encountered most of them in her years as a front-line royal. 'A great fount of wisdom for us all', said one of the family. Queen Mary

Surrounded by her family on her eighty-eighth birthday: The Queen, Viscount Linley; the Princess of Wales; Lady Sarah Armstrong-Jones. In the background is the Queen Mother's faithful steward William Tallon.

Four decades separate these pictures. The earlier photograph was taken in 1947 and the later one to celebrate the Queen Mother's birthday in 1985.

taught her about the old style of monarchy which her daughter-in-law never forgot. But she adapted this style to changing generations and fluctuating national fortunes – just as the Queen is doing now – and, in the process, became very much the power *beside* the throne. Suggestions that she was the stronger partner in the George and Elizabeth alliance have been made in the past but, in fact, it was a marriage of such concord that they balanced each other perfectly.

Elizabeth and her beloved Bertie most certainly achieved in their lives together everything the Archbishop of York directed them towards on their wedding day: 'You will have a great ambition to make this one life now given to you something rich and true and beautiful'. With his Queen by his side, King George grew into 'the great and noble King' so described by the Queen after his death in a moving statement in which she pledged to continue the work they had begun together.

Queen Elizabeth the Queen Mother's powerful influence in achieving that final glorious tribute is indisputable, just as her experience and guidance was of incalculable value to her daughter and the Prince of Wales – to whom his grandmother has been a guiding star all his life. He is quoted in *The Country Life Book of Queen Elizabeth the Queen Mother* by Godfrey Talbot as describing her as 'The most wonderful example of fun, laughter, warmth, infinite security and, above all else, exquisite taste in all things'. An assessment with which the Queen Mother's two daughters, six grandchildren, band of great-grandchildren and all her many 'honorary' British and Commonwealth family would whole-heartedly endorse.

CHAPTER 1

BIRTH OF A LEGEND

Queen Elizabeth, the Queen Mother aged six years.

CHAPTER 1

BIRTH OF A LEGEND

In the long lifetime that lay ahead of the baby girl born on a sweltering August bank holiday in London, man would travel to the moon and walk in space, invent a weapon capable of destroying the planet and prolong, improve and even create life through myriad medical breakthroughs.

But the world of Saturday, 4 August, 1900, in which the ninth child of Lord and Lady Glamis first opened those distinctive hyacinth blue eyes, was as yet unawakened to the wonder and menace of twentieth-century discoveries. Motor-cars were still a rarity, electricity yet to replace gas lamps, the Wright brothers first flight was still three years away and the telephone had not yet revolutionized communications.

The birth of a future Queen Empress of Britain and the Empire, as it still was, turned out to be a low-key affair – even for the daughter of the heir to an earldom. No fanfares or court circular announced the arrival of the baby who was destined to be daughter-in-law, sister-in-law, wife and mother to four sovereigns. Indeed her father treated the addition of a third surviving daughter to his family in such a relaxed fashion he did not even register her birth until 21 September when he was fined 7/6d for not reporting it sooner.

At secluded Osborne, on the Isle of Wight, where Queen Victoria was sinking into the decline that preceded the end five months later, the ailing Queen had just received news of the death of her second son 'Affie' Duke of Edinburgh and Saxe-Coburg. 'It is a horrible year, nothing but sadness and horrors', she lamented unaware of the new babe who would, one day, wed her five-year-old York great-grandson Prince Albert. He had visited her for both breakfast and tea only ten days before, on 25 July – one of her 'good days'. But over the grouse moors where shooting parties gathered later in the month for picnic lunches in the heather, word spread rapidly among the sixty-odd great families of turn-of-the-century Society, that 'Celia had another gel', born just before the seventeenth birthday of her elder sister Mary. Members of those families – Cecils, Howards, Bentincks, Russells, Cavendishes, Pelhams, Airlies, Buccleuchs and Ogilvies among them – had earlier 'seen in' the new century secure in the knowledge that Britons undeniably ruled the waves through a flourishing empire which stretched – to quote one newspaper of the day – 'round the globe, has one heart, one head, one language, one policy' and upon which 'the sun never set'. The immense power of the

Elizabeth aged two with the first of her many parasols. Later, as Duchess of York and then Queen, she made parasols a fashion accessory.

Elizabeth, aged two, with her elder sister Mary (who married Lord Elphinstone) at their rose-red Hertfordshire home, St Pauls, Walden Bury. Elizabeth always regarded '. . . Glamis as a holiday place – The Bury was home.'

select group of great families had yet to be partially eroded by the devastating effects of two world wars and taxation which trimmmed their riches forcing them to open their castles and mansions to the public for much needed revenue. Even the Queen Mother's old home in Scotland, Glamis Castle, has joined the growing band of stately homes seeking help with their upkeep. The Queen, also, opens part of her own two private homes – Balmoral and Sandringham – to sightseers.

No apprehension about the future troubled that gentle aristocrat 'Claudie', Lord Glamis, or clouded the enjoyment of his favourite month of August. Four years later he would inherit the Earldom of Strathmore and Kinghorne with all the attendant responsibilities. But now he did not linger with his wife and the new baby but hastened to Scotland where he was expected for the grouse shooting. In due course his family would join him for their summer holiday. While there he made nine runs in the Glamis v Strathmore cricket match, an annual event to which he looked forward eagerly. These pleasurable activities must have blurred his remembrance of his youngest daughter's place of birth and, as all Queen Elizabeth's six brothers and three sisters are now dead, there is no one to remember exactly where it took place.

The question only arose at the time of her eightieth birthday when she unveiled a plaque in the church of St Paul's Walden Bury, near her own home, commemorating her birth 'in this parish'. It then emerged that Her Majesty had not, in fact, been born there at all. Inquiries revealed that she is, almost certainly, a true Londoner. Born, if not within the sound of Bow Bells, then only a hansom cab drive away. Some reports even claim she was delivered in an ambulance somewhere in the vicinity of Hyde Park where carefree crowds enjoyed the bank holiday. It is possible, as there were some horse-drawn ambulances about, but unlikely, as births in 1900 rarely took place in hospital and Lady Glamis was not inexperienced in the business of childbirth. However, she was an up-to-date woman, well ahead of her time particularly in all matters relating to child-rearing, and may well have decided – at the age of thirty-seven after a seven-year interval between children – to have her accouchement in hospital. If so, she would have used the fashionable Bischoffsheim Ambulance Service, an innovation of Mr Thomas Ryan, the forward-thinking Secretary of St Mary's Paddington. So it is possible that the hospital where four of her great-grandchildren were born towards the end of the century, may also have been the Queen Mother's birthplace. No records exist to confirm this and the lack of evidence merely highlights the natural disinterest in her birth outside the family and their circle of friends. Where and how she arrived in the world, the Queen Mother herself does not appear to know. Alternatively, she may be displaying the understandable rectitude of her generation in a matter so personal. An attitude which could also explain her father's otherwise inexplicable mistake.

Whatever the circumstances the imperturbable Cecilia – before her marriage a Cavendish-Bentinck, kinswoman of the Duke of Portland – seems to have coped admirably with her ninth child. The first, a much-loved girl, had died tragically seven years before in a diphtheria epidemic, still a killer for that generation. Before long she and her baby were on their way to the peace and calm of 'The Bury', as the old rose-red, honeysuckle-hung house in Hertfordshire is known to the family. They left behind a London of top-hatted men and women in frilled bustles.

It would not be too long before hemlines would daringly creep just above the ankles and knickerbockers, for bicycling, became a very real threat to femininity – in the eyes of men.

Squally, rainy weather later that month took the place of the humid heatwave and newspaper headlines proclaimed 'Allies storm Pekin' as the fifty-six-day siege of the Boxer Rebellion in China, neared its end. In Glasgow, bubonic plague was reported; railway workers in South Wales ended their ten-day strike and Britain had its first taste of Coca-Cola – fourteen years after the United States. Abroad the Boer War, which had so distressed Queen Victoria, dragged interminably on, although news of the relief of Mafeking and Ladysmith earlier in the year had heartened those at home. In Marlborough House, Albert Edward, Prince of Wales, waited impatiently to ascend the throne as King Edward VII – he succeeded five months later at the beginning of 1901. At home, in the cosy nursery wing, Elizabeth Angela Marguerite, as she was christened on 23 September, was welcomed by her brothers and sisters: Mary Frances, John, Patrick, Alexander, Fergus, Rose and Michael. The first-born, Violet Hyacinth, had been buried in the village churchyard.

All upper-class Victorian and Edwardian houses had a comfortable nursery wing where 'Nanny' reigned supreme and the situation of baby Elizabeth was no exception. She loved the happy nursery environment so much she copied it almost exactly for her own children, Elizabeth and Margaret Rose – now the Queen and Princess Margaret,

The Bowes Lyon family in the early years of the century. Back row, from left to right: Fergus (later killed in the war); John; the 14th Earl of Strathmore; Mary; Patrick; Alexander (who died before the war). Front row, from left to right: Rose; Lady Strathmore with David on her knee; Elizabeth and Michael.

Lady Strathmore's 'two Benjamins'. Elizabeth ('Buffy') and her much-loved brother David. Usually so full of pranks, here they are looking exceptionally well behaved.

Countess of Snowdon – and the same nurse looked after them both.

Clara Cooper Knight (Allah) was a farmer's daughter from Hertfordshire who stayed with the family until Elizabeth was eleven. She remembered her as an 'exceptionally happy, easy baby; crawling early, running at thirteen months and speaking very young'. Two months later when she was toddling more steadily and beginning to discover the wonders of her mother's magnificent garden, Elizabeth's younger brother David was born on 2 May 1902. He was the last of the large family and arrived as Britain celebrated, at last, the end of the Boer War.

Because they were so close in age, their mother always referred to her last two children as 'my two Benjamins' after the Biblical story. They became inseparable as we learn from the Queen Mother's own memories written by her in the third person for a friend, Lady Cynthia Asquith:

> Her small brother David is always with her and usually a tiny Shetland pony called Bobs. Bobs will follow her into the house and even walk up and down long stone steps, and she has to be very careful that he doesn't tread on her little brother's toes.

During her childhood at 'The Bury', Elizabeth began a love affair with old houses and gardens which would be with her all her life. Here is her own description of it, again in the third person:

> At the bottom of the garden where the sun always seems to be shining is The Wood – the haunt of fairies, with its anemones and ponds and moss-grown statues and The Big Oak under which she reads and where the two ring doves Caroline Curly-Love and Rhoda Wrigley-Worm contentedly coo in their wicker-work Ideal Home. There are carpets of primroses and anemones to sit on, and she generally has tea either in the shadow of Diana or near another very favourite one called The Running Footman or the Bounding Butler (to grown-up people known as the Disc-Thrower).
>
> Whenever – and this is often – a dead bird is found in this enchanted wood it is given solemn burial in a small box lined with rose-leaves.

As they grew, two books for children – still favourite reading in royal nurseries – made their appearance. Beatrix Potter's *The Tale of Peter Rabbit* and Rudyard Kipling's *Just So* stories, both of which were read aloud by Lady Strathmore to her 'Benjamins'.

They were healthily mischievous children who used to hide from the grown-ups among the hens in 'The Flea House', a favourite place where they crouched in the hay giggling as their nurse searched for them in the grounds outside. In their hiding place they kept a store of forbidden 'goodies' as David Bowes Lyon remembered years later:

> Apples, oranges, sugar, sweets, slabs of chocolate Meunier, matches and packets of Woodbine. Many other things there were besides, and to this blissful retreat we used, between the ages of five and six, to have resource whenever it seemed an agreeable plan to escape our morning lessons.

In 1904, the year she was four – and Mr Rolls teamed up with Mr Royce to make motor-cars – her grandfather the 13th Earl of Strathmore and Kinghorne died. From a mere 'Honourable', she became the Lady Elizabeth, first step on a titular ladder that would see her elevated far beyond the reasonable expectations of an earl's daughter. At that time royal princes so close to the throne did not marry commoners, however ancient or distinguished their

A seventh birthday photograph of Elizabeth, her hair worn in the fringe that would one day be so fashionable when she became a royal duchess.

Elizabeth and David wearing clothes from an earlier century, dancing 'with admirable precision and grace' a stately measure of the eighteenth century.

pedigree. They married members of other royal families like Alexandra of Denmark ('The Sea-King's Daughter From Over The Sea') who wed the future King Edward VII.

With the earldom her father inherited Glamis Castle, beautifully situated in the shadow of the Grampian Mountains, near Dundee. It meant, each summer, the joyous adventure of travelling north by train for the Scottish holiday the Queen Mother so enjoys to this day. She still drives over from Balmoral to spend a night or two at the castle, sleeping in the chintzy pink bedroom where her second daughter Princess Margaret was born sixty years ago.

Elizabeth and David were pent up with excitement before the journey north. Glamis meant carefree holidays and 'The Flying Scot' was a magnificent chariot carrying them northwards. As it approached the border stop for water, they were allowed to lean out of the window and get their first appreciative sniff of fresh moorland air. Breakfast, as the train puffed on, seemed all the better for it.

Glamis Castle, ancestral home of the Bowes Lyons, is one of the oldest inhabited castles in Britain, said to be the setting for the murder of Duncan in *Macbeth.* It has been in the Queen Mother's family since Sir John Lyon – known as 'The White Lyon' because of his mane of flaxen hair – married King Robert II's daughter Jean in 1361. As her dowry he received the royal lands of Glamis and the barony of Kinghorne.

The Strathmores were deeply religious and every day there were household prayers. All the women in the family covered their heads with small lace caps and the staff – housemaids, housekeeper, butler, footmen, cook and kitchen maids – attended the service.

When Elizabeth and David arrived at Glamis for the holidays a whole new world opened up for them. There was always freedom in Scotland and they made friends of gamekeepers, foresters and the young rosy-cheeked maids in the dairy. Trotting on their ponies through the woods, learning about wildlife, flowers and trees from the people who worked among them, they were the happiest of children. Usually they were surrounded by animals of one sort or another. Dogs, cats, pigs, chickens, tortoises, ponies and pet doves made up a menagerie which the two 'Benjamins' adored and, where possible, followed them to Glamis.

A love of gardening that was to become an integral part of their lives – they both became Presidents of the Royal Horticultural Society – was nurtured at Glamis where Lady Strathmore was beginning to create a garden of great beauty. The castle itself is a forbidding place, believed to be the most haunted residence in the British Isles. 'Spooky but marvellous', as the Queen Mother recalls. As a child she became totally absorbed in the dark legends of her ancestors and later made an able guide for visitors; embellishing the blood-curdling stories with just the right blend of eeriness and drama. Her clear, precise young voice sank to a whisper or rose theatrically as she delighted in scaring visitors with a 'dummy' ghost she and David had made out of paper and laid in a dimly lit room.

Up the great, circular staircase where Macbeth carried the still-bleeding King Duncan – or so the story goes – the children played hide and seek. On the stone-flagged floor of King Duncan's Room, now covered, there was once, it is said, a large bloodstain. This was always pointed out to visitors with great relish by Elizabeth whose imagination, according to her brothers and sisters, was extremely vivid. Like all Edwardians they adored dressing-up. Clothes from many generations were kept in an old chest and produced on rainy afternoons or for a fancy-dress party. A visitor remembered an occasion when 'two little figures seemed to rise from the floor and dance with admirable precision and grace the stately measure so characteristic of the eighteenth century'.

But the two Benjamins were not always so civilized. Practical jokes were a speciality and Elizabeth was usually the ringleader. Unfortunate visitors often arrived at the

Elizabeth, aged nine, on her Shetland pony 'Bobs'. According to her own third person account: 'Bobs will follow her into the house and even walk up and down long stone steps and she has to be very careful that he doesn't tread on her little brother's toes.'

front door dripping water because the children had been playing a favourite game of 'repelling raiders' by pouring 'boiling oil' over the battlements. Another highly favoured game was covering themselves with feathers and pretending to be Red Indians on a raiding party. Startled dairy maids found themselves pounced on and threatened with 'scalping' unless they gave the two young rascals some fresh creamy milk and biscuits.

For a small child the future Queen had great self-possession which verged on precocity. But it was always laced with the appealing charm for which she is so loved. Much of this emanated from Lady Strathmore's attitude to her children. 'Life', she used to say, 'is for living and working at. If you find anything or anybody boring, the fault lies not in them but in you'. It was a philosophy the Queen Mother has followed all her life and has resulted in her happy knack of making each person to whom she is introduced feel they are just the one man or woman in the world she wanted to meet.

Unlike most youngsters in Edwardian Britain – most notably the restricted children of the Prince and Princess of Wales at York House – they were not confined to the nursery but could be with their parents whenever they wished. The Strathmores were both loving and approachable with a concept of life which embodied religion, duty and responsibility combined with warmth, humour and demonstrative affection towards their large family. The Duke and Duchess of York, soon to be King George V and Queen Mary, also instilled those principles into their growing family but lacked the ability to convey warmth and love.

In terms of upbringing the two families, later to be linked by marriage, adopted a quite different approach. The royal children grew up inhibited and starved of real love and affection. Prince Albert suffered from a serious speech defect and gastric problems due to being neglected by a nurse as a young child. The family of his future wife, however, were self-confident and natural and adhered to a code of conduct which made them both straightforward and unpretentious in their attitude to others.

As she spent so much time with her mother, Elizabeth learnt the art of being a good hostess at an early age. 'Shall us sit and talk?' she is credited with saying to a visitor at three years old. On another occasion her mother found her pouring out tea and chatting with great composure to some neighbours who had arrived early. The family always called for the youngest daughter if someone known to be difficult was expected. 'Let's ask Elizabeth. She can talk to anyone', her sister Rose once said.

This ability to put people at ease was demonstrated in a now historic gesture at a children's party when she was five. Vivid blue eyes looked compassionately at a boy of ten in a sailor suit. Bertie York, the King's grandson, was plainly both shy and ill at ease. So the kindly Elizabeth cheered him up by giving him the cherry off her piece of cake. This exceptional generosity so impressed the lad that he remembered it years later when he met her again.

Lady Strathmore herself gave the two Benjamins their first lessons – reading and writing – as Queen Elizabeth was to do herself with her own children. But as they grew up there came the inevitable parting of David and 'Buffy' as he always called his sister after early attempts to say 'Elizabuf'. He went away to school and she had the first of a series of governesses. Of one of them she wrote: 'Some governesses are nice and some are not!' One who was popular with Elizabeth was German-born Kathie Kuebler who described her charge as 'a small, delicate figure . . . a sensitive, somewhat pale little face, dark hair and very beautiful violet-blue eyes'. Another governess, Mademoiselle (christened Madé)Lang remembered her seven-year-old pupil having her fortune told by a gypsy. 'She read my hand', said the future Queen laughing, 'and said I'd be a queen when I grew up. Isn't it silly? Who wants to be a queen anyway.'

Elizabeth and David made up for their enforced separation with joyful reunions in the holidays. 'My sister and I used to go to the theatre as often as we were allowed', he told Lady Asquith. 'Usually to the cheaper seats as our purses never bulged. She had a wide taste in plays, but I think Barrie's were her favourites, though Shakespeare was by no means slighted'.

Once when they were particularly short of money, Elizabeth sent a telegram to her father at Glamis: 'SOS. LSD. RSVP. Elizabeth'.

On 6 May 1910, King Edward VII died. At the funeral at Windsor the German Kaiser – so soon to be an enemy – complained because he had to give precedence to a dog. The late King's fox terrier Caesar walked dolefully behind the flag-draped coffin. Elizabeth heard the grown-ups talking about the King's death. But to an impressionable youngster the death of the great nurse Florence Nightingale three months later made a deeper impact, particularly as her elder sister Rose planned to be a nurse.

A year later the Strathmores were grieving for their middle son Alexander (Alec) who died at Glamis aged twenty-four. It was a sad prelude to the second decade in the Queen Mother's life; one that would have more than its natural allotment of tragedy, and dark days, as the young Elizabeth matured early to demonstrate a fine sense of responsibility and service.

CHAPTER 2
GROWING UP

The first of many portraits. Mabel Hankey painted this watercolour study of Elizabeth aged eight, little knowing that the pensive youngster with the long, dark hair would grow up to be a queen.

CHAPTER 2

GROWING UP

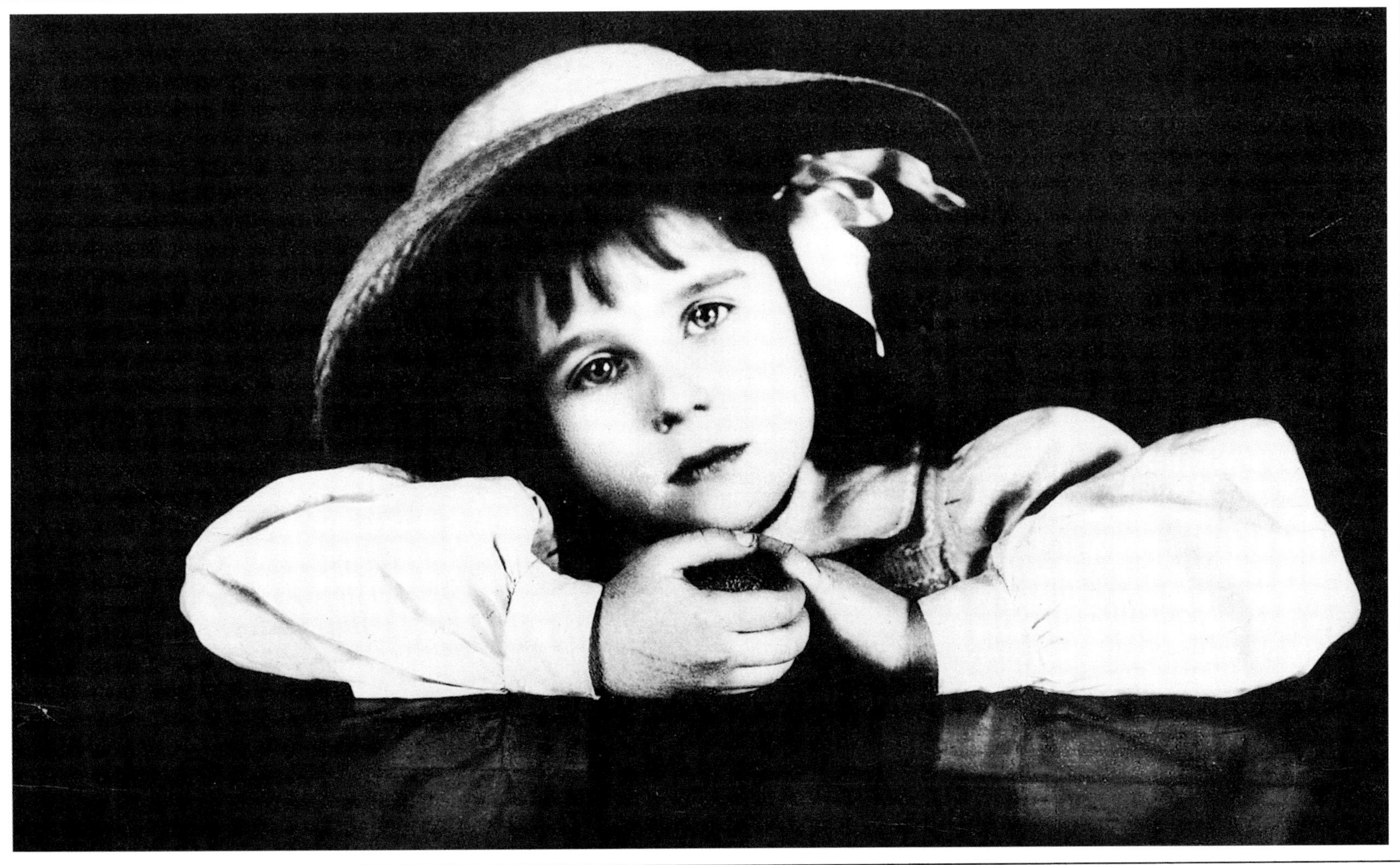

THE Strathmores had little to do with the Court of Edward VII. As a young man in the Life Guards doing his stint of duty at Windsor Castle, the Earl had disliked what he saw of the racy life of the then Prince of Wales. The Court he later surrounded himself with as King held little attraction for 'Claudie' and 'Celia' as the Earl and Countess were known to family and friends. Perhaps unconsciously – for they were immensely patriotic – they distanced themselves from 'Tum Tum', as the King was nicknamed because of his gourmandizing, and his courtiers. They brought their children up far from the fashionable life of the day and the scandals of 'The King's Set'.

But the accession of George V and Queen Mary bred a Court of a very different calibre. It would eventually bring

Elizabeth, when aged twelve, visited her aunt, Lady Cavendish, at the Villa Poggio Ponente at Bordighera.

Lady Elizabeth with her elder sister Rose (later Countess Granville) talking to a wounded soldier at Glamis. The soldiers joked that when they went back to the trenches they would wear labels saying 'Send back to Glamis Castle' in case they were wounded again.

royalty once again to Glamis, through their neighbour, the Countess of Airlie, great friend and lady-in-waiting to the new Queen. As a magazine of the day pontificated: 'The Court today at Windsor is to an extraordinary extent a reproduction of the Court as it existed in the Fifties. It is a Court which is primarily a family – there is no 'bridge' nor any of the fashionable dissipation so dear to the Smart Set'.

Outside the sober and restrained royal circle, the mood was one of great excitement as London prepared for the coronation on 23 June 1911. The late Sir Osbert Sitwell, poet, novelist, writer on Edwardian society and a great friend of the Queen Mother, recalled those pre-1914 days when 'an air of gaiety unusual in northern climes prevailed. Music flowed with the lightness and flash of water under the striped awnings and from the balconies; while beyond the open illuminated windows, the young men about to be slaughtered still feasted unconscious of all but the moment'.

In the schoolroom at 20 St James's Square, where the Strathmores had their town house, eleven-year-old Elizabeth wrote to her 'darling brother' David away at school. She told him about the decorations that festooned the nearby Mall and the rehearsals for the processions, particularly the famous team of eight cream horses from the royal mews which drew the State coach.

That summer's 'Coronation Fever' infected Britons in different ways. The butchers' trade journal rather naturally deplored that meat sales were down, commenting that 'vegetarianism is spreading over the country like some loathesome disease'. The women's suffrage movement organized their greatest-ever procession with 40,000 women parading to the Albert Hall – a spectacle which would have amazed Queen Victoria's Prince Consort to whose memory the memorial was erected.

In the Mall, as the Royal Family enjoyed afternoon tea with the many European relatives who had arrived for the coronation, an old lady determined to see the spectacle, settled herself on the pavement for a long wait. She had, very sensibly, brought with her a spirit lamp and kettle with which to brew her tea – an item which Elizabeth's father would have read in *The Times* the following day.

After the coronation Londoners continued to enjoy themselves with the recklessness which often affects those on the brink of crisis. It was the beginning of ragtime and American vaudeville artist Shirley Kellog was the toast of the town in her hit show *Hello Ragtime* at the Hippodrome. At the London Coliseum, acts from all over Europe were delighting audiences with rumbustuous vaudeville. Elizabeth was taken to see it for her fourteenth birthday treat and it was an anniversary she always remembered for it changed her pleasant, ordered life completely. At half past ten that evening Germany declared war on Britain. The Kaiser would henceforth be an enemy of his grandmother's people. From the theatre box, surrounded by her family, Elizabeth sang the national anthem with an emotional audience. Later, on the way home to 20 St James's Square, it would be tempting to speculate that they went via Buckingham Palace where huge crowds cheered King George and Queen Mary. It would have been one of the few times in her long life that Queen Elizabeth stood outside the Palace at a time of national crisis. As King George wrote in his diary that night: 'The cheering was terrific'.

The birthday evening at the theatre was one of the last times the whole family were together. The three eldest

brothers, Patrick, John (Jock) and Fergus, joined their regiment, the Black Watch. Michael left university for the Royal Scots.

Suddenly there was one wedding after another: Fergus to Lady Christian Dawson-Damer; Jock to the Honourable Fenella Hepburn-Stuart-Forbes-Trefusis. Lady Strathmore hurriedly shopped in London 'for outfits of every sort of medicine' as Elizabeth told Lady Asquith. 'And to the gunsmiths to buy all the things that people thought they wanted for a war, and found they didn't'.

The following week they travelled to Glamis – strangely silent for August with all the menfolk away. There were no cricket matches or shooting parties; only workmen already beginning to convert the castle into a hospital. The billiard table was piled high with 'comforts' for the troops; thick wool socks, mufflers, shirts and sweaters. Beds lined the dining-room waiting for the first injured to arrive from France. The crypt, complete with ancient axes, suits of armour and hunting trophies, was furnished as their dining-room. In the Queen Mother's own words: 'Lessons were neglected, for during those first few months we were so busy knitting, knitting, knitting and making shirts for the local battalion – the Black Watch. My chief occupation was crumpling up tissue paper until it was so soft that it no longer crackled to put in the lining of sleeping bags'.

That first wartime Christmas she helped decorate a huge tree from the estate and wrapped up parcels for the soldiers who had arrived from the trenches. Lady Strathmore was determined to make their Christmas away from home a happy one and stifled thoughts of her own sons in the fighting lines. Elizabeth waited every day with her spaniel Peter by the canon outside the castle, hoping to catch a glimpse of the postman with letters from France. 'She had the loveliest pair of blue eyes I'd ever seen – very expressive, eloquent eyes that could speak for themselves', one of the soldiers remembered. 'She was very fond of cycling about the grounds, often with both

Ancient Glamis Castle, the Strathmore's family home in Scotland. In the First World War it was converted to a military hospital.

her eyes tight shut and I've seen her roll off, spring up, grab her sun bonnet and jump on again, laughing and enjoying my fright immensely'.

Like other families the Strathmores lived in dread of a telegram from the War Office which finally came in September 1915. Fergus, who had been home on leave only a few days before to celebrate his first wedding anniversary with his young wife and meet his baby daughter, had been killed in the battle of Loos. One of the soldiers recalled: 'This bombshell threw the castle into deep sorrow and gloom and us boys felt very keenly for our sweet hostess, His Lordship and the family'. Elizabeth coped with the loss of a second brother in four years, helped by the natural resilience of youth. But she looks back on 'those awful years' every Armistice Day as she stands on the balcony in Whitehall, opposite the Cenotaph, with the rest of the Royal Family.

A grieving Lady Strathmore was given great strength by Elizabeth who stepped in to bridge the emotional gap between the family and the soldiers, guests under their roof, who wanted so much to help. She amused the boys in hospital blue because she was so terrified of mice. They told her she should see the size of the rats in the trenches. She would sit at the piano, playing to them and singing the nostalgic songs of those times: *It's a long way to Tipperary*, *Goodbye Dolly* (from the Boer War) and *There's a long road a winding*. She went to the village shop with Peter, the spaniel, to buy Woodbines, Gold Flake and Navy Cut and played endless games of whist or wrote letters home for the patients. The soldiers used to joke that when they returned to duty they would wear labels, in case they were injured again, which read: 'Please return to Glamis Castle'.

In the same year that Fergus was killed, another British serviceman who immortalized all those who lost their lives, died on active service. Rupert Brooke's legacy was *The Soldier*, a poem that still brings tears to the Queen Mother's eyes.

It was 1916 and the news from France was disastrous. The biggest British army yet sent into battle was decimated in the Battle of the Somme. Familiar names stared out of *The Times* lists of the 60,000 casualties, sixty per cent of which were among the officer ranks.

On her seventeenth birthday, having grown up rapidly during the war, Elizabeth felt eligible to put her hair up. As the first American forces landed in France, giving a much-needed boost to morale, she declared herself no longer a 'flapper' – the nickname given to young girls whose hair 'flapped about'. Already she had more than average responsibility. Lady Strathmore's health had deteriorated since the war and she never really recovered from the shock of Fergus's death. Then Michael too was reported killed, something his younger brother David refused to believe. He came home from Eton without a black arm-band or tie. 'Michael is not dead! I have seen him twice. He is in a big house surrounded by fir trees. I think he is very ill. I don't care what the War Office says, I know he is alive', insisted David. The Strathmores, like some Celtic families, have, on occasion, been credited with the gift of second sight. David is believed to have possessed 'the giftie' and, in this case, he was happily proved right. Michael arrived home several months later to confirm that he had, indeed, been in a house surrounded by fir trees with a very bad head wound.

Elizabeth's other brother Patrick also had a narrow escape from death after he had been badly wounded in heavy fighting. As Queen Mother, she met the man who rescued him when she visited the 'Old Contemptibles' in London. Jack Campbell, now ninety-four was the Army Medical Corps private who dragged Captain Bowes Lyon to safety.

In 1917, after three years of war against Germany, George V proclaimed that the name of Windsor would, in future, be borne by his family and not the former German titles. Although it meant little to Elizabeth at the time, this proclamation would have a significant effect on her future life.

Rose Bowes Lyon, who was ten years older than Elizabeth and a trained nurse, had run the hospital when her mother became unwell. But when she married Commander William Leveson-Gower, later Lord Granville, much of the responsibility was shouldered by her younger sister. It was an unusual training for a future queen but one that surely could not have been bettered, for it gave her Kipling's 'common touch' and accustomed her to a life of service. She saw all facets of human nature in the men fresh from the horrors of war in the trenches. Their optimism, hopelessness, terror and courage allied to a background of family suffering, were impressed upon the young girl's formative mind.

In retrospect the Queen Mother recognizes the value of those years when, above all, the example of her remarkable mother was paramount. In that atmosphere she grew up rapidly in terms of human experience. At eighteen, when the war ended, on 11 November 1918, she was mature beyond her years.

CHAPTER 3

MARRIAGE AND MOTHERHOOD

Something from her former life: a treasured teddy bear gets a hug from a radiantly happy Elizabeth.

OPPOSITE: *Marriage, especially to a royal prince, is a serious business, as Elizabeth shows in this pre-wedding picture with her father, the Earl of Strathmore, and her eldest brother Lord Glamis.*

CHAPTER 3

MARRIAGE AND MOTHERHOOD

THE New Year of 1920 'was hailed in London with a rattle of jazz drums and a frenzy of syncopation', reported the *Evening Standard* next morning.

For Elizabeth Bowes Lyon, her dark hair teased into a fringe above those remarkable blue eyes, the change of pace from the peace of Glamis could not have been more emphatic. The year before she had been busy in the hospital looking after the last of the wounded and helping to rehabilitate them. She was also working, with increasing enthusiasm, for the Forfarshire Girl Guides of which she later became District Commissioner. Lady Airlie noted she was 'very unlike the cocktail drinking, chain-smoking girls who came to be regarded as typical of the 1920s. Her radiant vitality and a blending of gaiety, kindness and sincerity made her irresistible to men'.

It was, indeed, a heady mixture but it was, perhaps, more important that Elizabeth in her poke-bonnet hats and old-fashioned homespun skirts typified normality in reckless, post-war Britain. She did not soak her handkerchief in morphine to sniff before a dance as was the practice of her contemporaries, smoke de Reszke cigarettes through a long holder or toss back 'White Lady' cocktails. Concern was mounting that shorter skirts meant lower morals. The men back from the trenches had fun with the short-skirted, silk-stockinged 'good sports' but they fell in love with girls like Elizabeth Bowes Lyon with her gentleness and beautiful manners. Which was probably why she kept the King's second son waiting for three long years before becoming his wife. She was, quite simply, having a marvellous time.

He saw her, in time-honoured fashion, across a crowded dance floor at the Ritz, dancing with his equerry James Stuart, the future Earl of Moray. Or it could have been at Lord and Lady Farquhar's ball that Bertie uttered the immortal words to Jamie Stuart: 'Thats a lovely girl you've been dancing with – who is she?' Accounts differ

An engagement portrait of the future Duchess of York by John St Helier. She is wearing a long brocade coat with a white ermine collar over a blue silk taffeta dress.

and the Queen Mother herself remains discreet about the momentous day when the King's second son fell deeply in love and changed her life completely. Since then she has willingly given up so much of her privacy and believes quite rightly that the most personal of her memories should remain so. But it is clear that Prince Albert, who had been created Duke of York in June, was not, at first, a successful suitor. He suffered from the eternal problem of the second child brought up in the shadow of a more sparkling elder sibling. At that time his brother's brilliant flame all but extinguished the flickering spark which kindled into an inspirational torch for a nation at war twenty years later. But as a young man, David who would be, briefly, King Edward VIII, then Duke of Windsor, was far more extrovert, dashing and sophisticated. Bertie had been cruelly treated as a child by an unbalanced nurse who bullied him and probably caused the bad stutter he developed at the age of seven. She also fed him eratically with poor-quality food which resulted in chronic digestive trouble for the rest of his life. But it was the stammer when nervous that was the outstanding problem – the one everyone noticed. In addition there were the moods of irritation and deep depression which punctuated his adolescence and occasionally visited him in later years.

Because of his hesitation and introvert manner, the King feared his son might be 'slow'. But Lady Airlie, Queen Mary's lady-in-waiting and the Strathmore's neighbour at Cortachy Castle, thought differently. That shrewd and perceptive woman probed gently beneath the surface of the Prince to find 'that far from being backward he was an intelligent child with more force of character than anyone suspected in those days'. But the qualities that would eventually emerge to make George VI a fine and courageous King were not apparent in 1920 when Elizabeth again met the Prince she had first met at that childhood party many years before.

Earlier in the year Lord and Lady Strathmore held a coming out dance for their daughter which she nearly missed because of a high temperature. But with the resolution that would mark her attitude to her future public engagements, she insisted on leading the dancing, looking particularly beautiful despite a rosy flush of fever. Family friend Lady Buxton noted: 'Elizabeth Lyon is out now and Cecilia had a dance for her. How many hearts Elizabeth will break'. The 'hearts' were already lining up to be counted – among them a royal one. As one admirer put it: 'I fell madly in love. They all did'.

In America prohibition was tightening its grip and in Britain unemployment topped a million as ex-soldiers struggled to make new lives for themselves. Bitter opposition greeted Dr Marie Stopes when she opened Britain's first birth-control clinic in London for women who did not want to bring babies into the brave new world of the twenties. The Duke of York felt deeply about unemployment and began a life-long interest in boys' clubs and industrial welfare.

In his personal life the long drawn out wooing proceeded through orthodox channels, in accordance with most royal courtships. His sister Princess Mary was very friendly with Elizabeth through their mutual interest in Guiding. Later on, in February 1922, she helped the romance to develop by making Elizabeth one of the bridesmaids when she married Viscount Lascelles. Meanwhile Bertie found himself integrated into the happy, relaxed atmosphere of summer at Glamis which someone once described as 'like living in a Van Dyke picture. Time and the gossiping, junketing world stood still'. Elizabeth accentuated the timelessness of the castle by appearing at a dinner before the Forfar Ball in 1920 in a Vandyke-styled dress of deep rose brocade with pearls entwined in her hair. Round the dining room – so recently a hospital ward – kilted pipers marched, bagpipes swirling as the old custom of playing after dinner was revived.

The Duke found his life transformed. Although reasonably happy and cordial on the surface, the Royal Family's home life was repressed, cold and excessively formal. To be suddenly part of the Bowes Lyon clan, if only as a guest, brought warmth, affection and natural spontaneity into his life for the first time. They laughed a lot at Glamis; sang round the piano and played charades – very much as the Royal Family relax today.

The Duke was enchanted but found that Elizabeth had many suitors who were equally besotted. Over at Balmoral Queen Mary was intrigued after receiving a letter from Bertie: 'It is delightful here', he wrote, 'and Elizabeth is very kind to me. The more I see of her the more I like her'. Her Majesty installed herself at convenient Cortachy with Lady Airlie from whence she sallied forth to Glamis to inspect the youngest daughter of the castle.

Lady Strathmore was ill and Elizabeth's talent as a hostess flowered in the royal presence. The Queen was impressed and decided she was 'the one girl who could make Bertie happy'.

The first links in the royal chain that would bond Elizabeth to the service of the British nation for the rest of her life had been forged. She was just twenty years old and the familiar world she knew was at her feet. It is understandable there was considerable hesitation before her wings were clipped permanently. 'She was frankly doubtful', wrote Lady Airlie in her memoirs, 'uncertain of her feelings and afraid of the public life which would lie ahead of her as the King's daughter-in-law'. Of the Duke, she wrote: 'He was deeply in love but so humble'. The King, who 'disapproved of modern girls with their painted

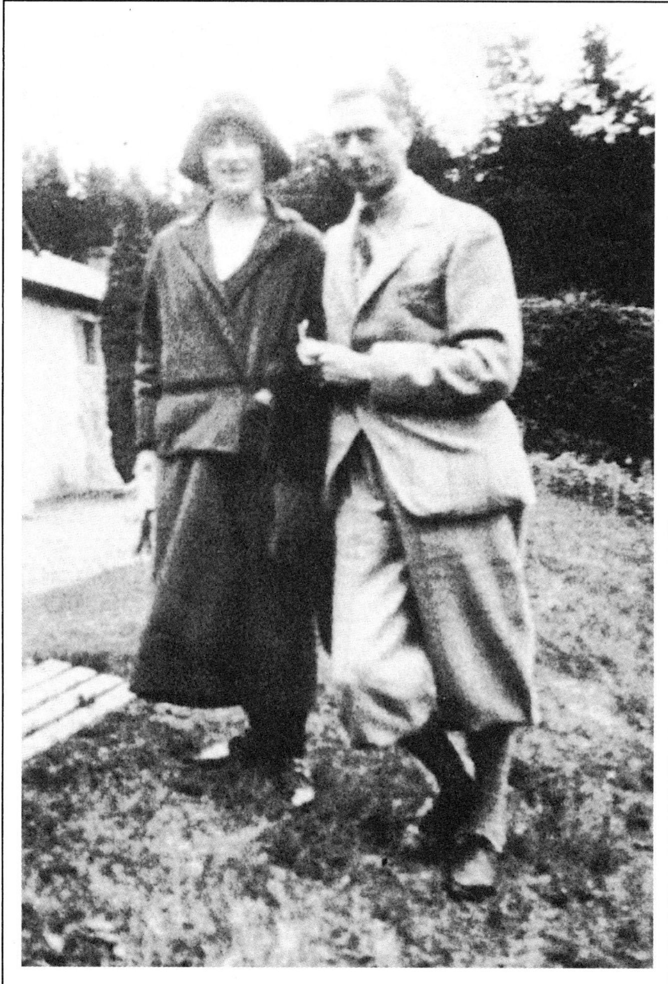

From the Duke of Windsor's private albums: Elizabeth and 'Bertie' relaxing together (left); the first and only picture of the Queen Mother smoking – but only in jest.

finger nails', as his son David wrote years later in *A King's Story*, was keen on the match. But pessimistic: 'You'll be a lucky fellow, Bertie, if she accepts you', he counselled.

It is not clear when and how the first proposal was made. But it was the custom, firmly approved of by George V, for royal proposals to be conducted through an emissary so that the royal personage concerned would be spared the indignity of a refusal. Viscount Davidson mentioned in his memoirs that the Duke of York had told him this and 'worse still I gather that an emissary had already been sent to ascertain whether the girl was prepared to marry him and that it had failed. The question was: what was he to do?' According to Davidson, he told the Duke that, in 1922, 'no high-spirited girl of character was likely to accept a proposal made at second hand. If she was as fond of him as he thought she was he must propose to her himself'.

Whatever the circumstances, Elizabeth certainly refused two proposals but accepted the third – which Bertie did make himself – a not unexpected reaction from that particular 'high-spirited girl'. But there were two weary years for the Duke to wait before he was successful. Lady Strathmore, Lady Airlie and Queen Mary were understandably disappointed at the first refusal. Elizabeth's mother wrote sagely and with more significance than she realized, to Lady Airlie: 'I do hope he will find a nice wife who will make him happy. I like him so much and he is a man who will be made or marred by his wife'.

It is all such ancient history now – the doubts and misgivings of a young girl who overcame them to become wife and mother of a sovereign and a universal 'grandmother' to millions. 'I said to him I was afraid, as royalty, never never again to be free to think or speak or act as I feel I ought to think or speak or act', were her own words spoken to a close friend. They summed up everything a commoner feels about marrying into the Royal Family and are the reason the Queen Mother knows so well how her granddaughters-in-law, Diana and Sarah, sometimes feel.

Princess Alice, granddaughter of Queen Victoria, believed that 'none but those trained from youth to such

Four days before this photograph was taken to celebrate her engagement, Elizabeth had said 'yes' to 'Bertie', Duke of York, the King's second son in the 'Enchanted Wood' of her childhood at St Pauls, Walden Bury.

an ordeal can sustain it with amiability and composure'. Princess Alice of Gloucester, the Queen Mother's sister-in-law, put it another way. She wrote in her memoirs that in marrying a royal prince she had to accept 'that I was a servant of the country'.

At the start of 1923, the Duke of York was still hoping Elizabeth Bowes Lyon would marry him. Lady Airlie, firmly on his side, quietly persevered in her efforts to encourage the Strathmore's youngest daughter. 'One knew instinctively that she was a girl who would find real happiness only in marriage and motherhood. A born home-maker', she concluded.

Her mother noticed that Elizabeth showed signs of worry. 'I think she was torn between her longing to make Bertie happy and her reluctance to take on the responsibilities this marriage must bring', she said. The diarist Chips Channon,[1] who was a little in love with her himself, also saw how troubled Elizabeth was that winter. 'She certainly has something on her mind . . . she is more gentle, lovely and exquisite than any woman alive, but this evening I thought her unhappy and distraite'.

Early in January, 1923, Lady Airlie, encouraged no doubt by Queen Mary, determined on one last attempt to convince Elizabeth. She invited her to tea and talked about the problems of her own married life and the eventual 'mutually rewarding, loving partnership'. It was not the sort of confidence normally exchanged over the teacups in their sort of circle. But it gave Elizabeth a new insight into marriage and may even have influenced her decision a few days later when Bertie arrived for the weekend. This time, at The Bury, he certainly made the proposal himself, on Sunday 13 January. Led by Elizabeth the couple visited the Enchanted Wood of her childhood which held some of her happiest memories. So propitious was the setting, and the moment, that – according to her friend Lady Cynthia Asquith – 'before they left this glamorous wood where the sun always seemed to be shining, the Prince had declared his suit and the youngest daughter in England's latest fairy story had joyfully consented to begin to live happily ever after'.

A jubilant Duke of York sent a telegram to his parents at Sandringham: 'All right. Bertie'. It was his pre-arranged signal that the royal marriage was on. The betrothal was made public two days later and as Elizabeth wrote to a friend: 'The cat is now completely out of the bag and there is no possibility of stuffing him back!'

She began to learn, as her granddaughters-in-law Diana and Sarah have done in recent years, about life behind that 'glass curtain' there would always be in future between herself and the 'dear public'. Royalty does not have intimate friends, she discovered, unless they were courtiers like Lady Airlie and utterly trusted. Confrontation on any established issue, as laid down first by Queen Victoria and later by Queen Mary, was extremely unwise. Elizabeth learnt that it was not so much 'catching the eye' after dinner but the long ceremony of the Queen buttoning on her elbow-length white gloves, which was the signal for the ladies to withdraw, first curtsying to the King. As Princess Alice of Gloucester puts it in her memoirs: 'The Court was much more formal. One was expected to change for tea and again for dinner which called for gloves and jewellery. Tiaras were worn frequently'.

In the world outside Coco Chanel, once an orphaned peasant girl, launched Chanel No 5 perfume and decreed sweaters were chic. The Chanel look that is still with us was born. There were no Paris fashions for the royal bride who was deeply conscious of the growing unrest and poverty in post-war Britain. She asked for no lavish wedding presents, but the King and Queen ignored this and gave her an ermine cape. They also showered her with fabulous jewellery – some of it heirlooms from the 'jewel-pool', as it is called in the Royal Family today. Herbert Asquith, later Lord Oxford and Asquith, invited to view the wedding presents, commented grumpily: 'Not a thing did I see that I should have cared to have or give'. He added: 'The poor little bride was completely overshadowed'. If Asquith was right, it was for the first and last time. Elizabeth blossomed immediately as Duchess of York and the King was as great an admirer as anyone. Even the staid old 'Times' grew positively lyrical: 'She has wonderful skin and hair. But her greatest charm is her voice. It is like cream and honey turned into sound and the listener is hypnotised by its musical quality.'

It is difficult to believe the sane and sensible Cecilia Strathmore enjoyed this type of saccharin. Her dry comment to a friend: 'Some people, dear, have to be fed royalty like sea lions with fish', shows how much she disliked sycophancy. Admiral Beatty's bluff sailor's description of Elizabeth as 'a perfect little duck' would have been more to her taste.

'Chose yourself a wife who you will always and only love', was the advice of the first Poet Laureate John Skelton to the future Henry VIII who, unfortunately, did not take it. The Duke of York most certainly would have done had it been offered to him. But he managed well enough without it, adoring his wife who became the cornerstone of his life. She, in her turn, grew to love him deeply. 'They were perfect together', said one of her sisters.

Soon after the engagement was announced, Elizabeth gave her first and last newspaper interview to Mr Harry Cozens-Hardy of *The Star* who, on the optimistic premise that it was worth trying, turned up on the doorstep of 17 Bruton Street. 'Leave this gentleman to me', Elizabeth

told the hitherto formidable Lady Strathmore. When asked the sixty-four-dollar question of why she had refused the Duke of York twice before accepting him, she turned those magnificent, dark-lashed eyes on Mr Cozens-Hardy and said: 'Now look at me. Do you think I am the sort of person Bertie would have to ask twice?' As an exercise in diplomacy it could not be faulted. In retrospect, it also suggests that Viscount Davidson's advice to the Duke was taken and when he asked her himself, the answer was 'Yes'.

The King was horrified by the interview, however tactful. Royal ladies did not speak to the press and he sent an equerry to tell Elizabeth so.

But in reality she could do little wrong in George V's eyes. In his diary he wrote: 'Bertie is a very lucky fellow'. When she arrived late for a meal, the King – a stickler for punctuality – merely said: 'Don't worry my dear. We must have sat down a few minutes early'. Few men who have encountered the Queen Mother at any stage of her life have not fallen a little in love with her and the King was

The formal wedding group at Buckingham Palace. Beside the royal couple are the Earl and Countess of Strathmore (left) and King George V and Queen Mary.

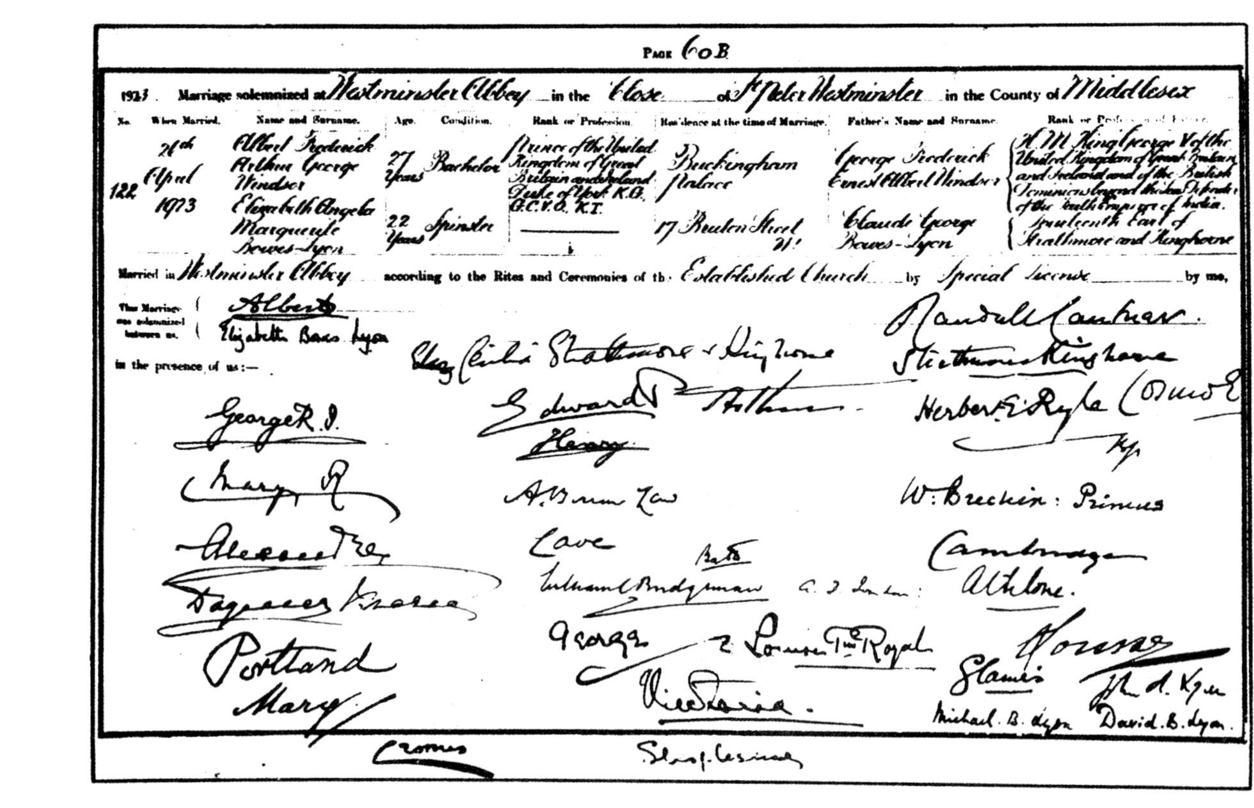

Page 60B

1923. Marriage solemnized at Westminster Abbey in the Close of St Peter Westminster in the County of Middlesex

No.	When Married.	Name and Surname.	Age.	Condition.	Rank or Profession.	Residence at the time of Marriage.	Father's Name and Surname.	Rank or Profession of Father.
122	26th April 1923	Albert Frederick Arthur George Windsor	27 Years	Bachelor	Prince of the United Kingdom of Great Britain and Ireland Duke of York K.G. G.C.V.O. K.T.	Buckingham Palace	George Frederick Ernest Albert Windsor	H M King George V of the United Kingdom of Great Britain and Ireland and of the British Dominions beyond the Seas Emperor of India.
		Elizabeth Angela Marguerite Bowes-Lyon	22 Years	Spinster	———	17 Bruton Street W.	Claude George Bowes-Lyon	Fourteenth Earl of Strathmore and Kinghorne

Married in Westminster Abbey according to the Rites and Ceremonies of the Established Church by Special Licence by me,

This Marriage was solemnized between us, Albert, Elizabeth Bowes Lyon

in the presence of us:—

Randall Cantuar.
Strathmore Kinghorne
George R.I.
Edward P
Arthur
Herbert E. Ryle
Henry
Mary R
A. Bonar Law
W. Brechin: Primus
Alexandra
Cave
Cambridge
Athlone
George
Louise Princess Royal
Portland
Glamis
Mary
Victoria
Michael B. Lyon
David B. Lyon
Cromer

The new royal Duchess signs her old name for the last time on the marriage certificate. Note the absence of a hyphen, often incorrectly attributed to her surname.

no exception. For her part she was really fond of the gruff, irascible old man. It had been part of Lady Strathmore's training to find something interesting in everyone and her daughter was fascinated by this new father-in-law who also happened to be her sovereign.

Once her decision to marry Bertie was made, Elizabeth threw all her worries aside and looked radiantly happy. Her mother remembered how, as a small girl, she had overheard a conversation between two women about a friend who was marrying 'but only for his position and money'. Reproachfully the young Elizabeth interrupted them: 'Perhaps someone will marry him 'cos she loves him'.

For their wedding in Westminster Abbey – which was not broadcast because churchmen feared that 'disrespectful men in pubs might listen with their hats on' – Elizabeth wore a simple gown of ivory silk crêpe banded with silver lamé, pearls and subtly gleaming beads, with sleeves of Nottingham lace which gave British lace-makers a much-needed boost. Her veil of antique Point de Flandres lace was lent by Queen Mary.

Lady Elizabeth, still a commoner, made the journey to the Abbey in an ordinary landau with her father splendidly attired in his Lord Lieutenant's crimson. For the return journey as a royal Duchess with the Duke by her side, she travelled for the first time in a red and gold State coach with an imposing escort of the Household Cavalry.

As Londoners made a gigantic holiday of the wedding, they little realized they were celebrating the marriage of a future King and Queen. Holding her new husband's hand beneath the rug protecting them from the chilly April breezes, Elizabeth used the other one to give a foretaste of her now famous wave: 'like unscrewing one of those giant jars of sweets', she now says to young emerging royals, as she shows them how it is done.

Part of their honeymoon was spent at Glamis where much of her trousseau had been made by local seamstresses. There Elizabeth contracted whooping cough – 'so unromantic to catch whooping cough on your honeymoon', wrote the disconsolate Duke to the King and Queen.

Tended by the local doctor and her mother, the bride soon recovered in time to go on to Frogmore, near Windsor, for the remainder of her honeymoon. To amuse her, the Duke may well have told her the story of his family kneeling in prayer in the adjacent mausoleum on the anniversary of great-grandmother Victoria's death. A dove flew above them. 'Dear Mama's spirit', suggested

Queen Alexandra. 'I am sure it is not', said the more realistic Princess Louise. 'Dear Mama's spirit would never have ruined Beatrice's hat'.

As the honeymooners relaxed, King George V's Britain continued to make news copy. If inclined, they would have read in the newspapers that Hobbs had scored his 100th century, joining the select band of 'Century Centurions'. And at Wembley, on Cup Final day, just before the King's arrival, a lone policeman on a white horse courageously prevented a disaster by calmly coaxing back crowds who had surged on to the pitch.

Queen Mary, meanwhile, had been happily preparing their first home – gaslit White Lodge in Richmond Park. While her mother-in-law had fond memories of the old house which had been her childhood home, Elizabeth had an equally happy remembrance of her childhood in St James's Square. She longed for a base in London and was delighted when her sister-in-law, Princess Mary, offered them the loan of Chesterfield House, not far from Buckingham Palace.

Settling down to married life, both Elizabeth and Bertie flourished. When he was with her the Duke cast off his

Sensible country clothes for the newly-weds at Polesden Lacey, near Dorking, Surrey, where the first part of the honeymoon was spent.

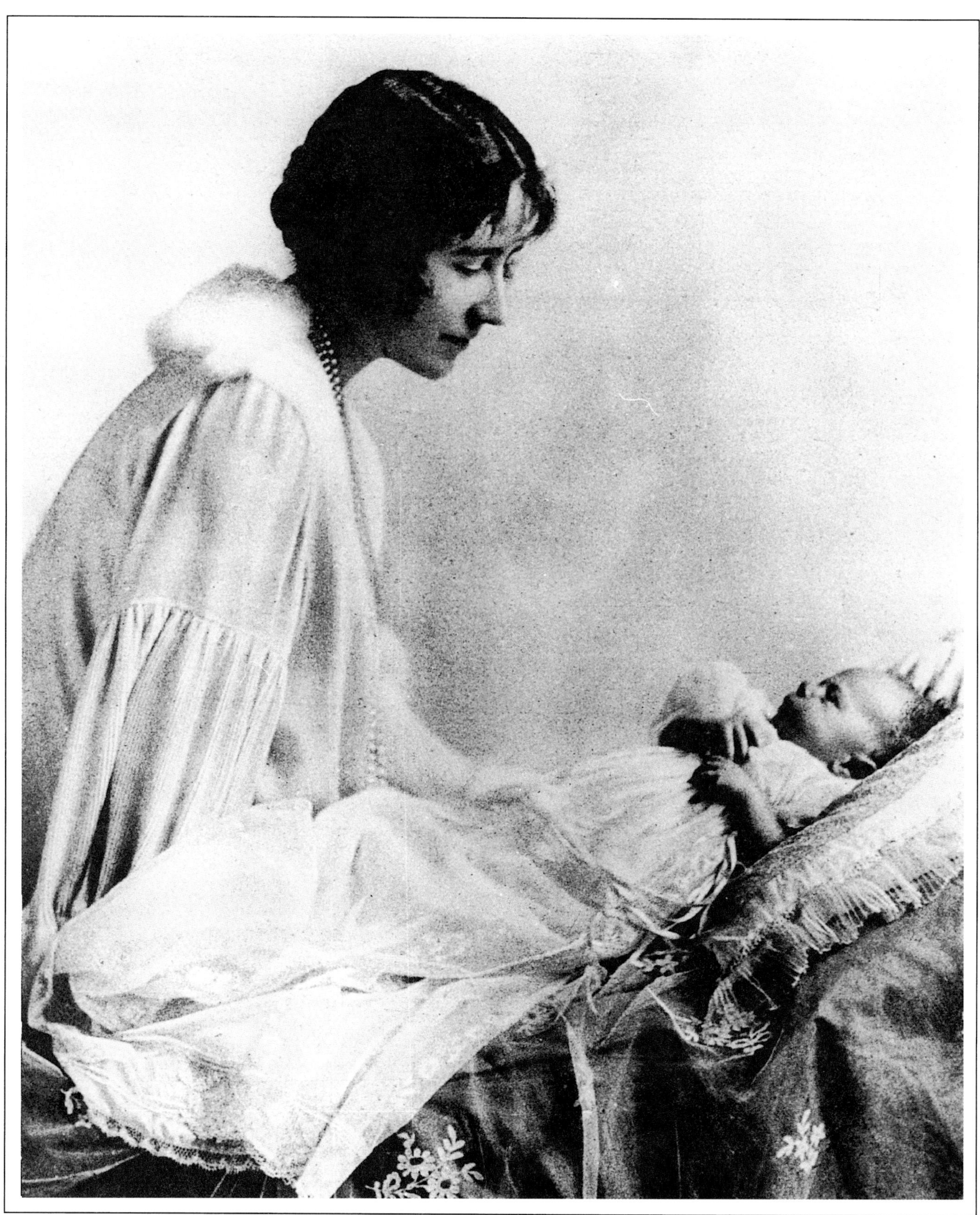

Two future Queens. The Duchess of York, later Queen Consort of George VI, looks lovingly down at the future Elizabeth II.

nervousness and reserve and his full potential soon became more evident. But there was still the problem of his speech impediment. The young Duchess heard of a speech therapist called Lionel Logue who was to play his part in the making of the future King George VI. 'He entered my consulting room at 3 o'clock in the afternoon, a slim, quiet young man, with tired eyes and all the outward signs of a man upon whom habitual speech defect had begun to set the sign. When he left at 5 o'clock you could see there was hope once more in his heart'. Logue taught the Duke the correct way to breathe which, he said, was the root of his problem. The Yorks practised together and he gradually began to improve.

The December after their wedding they had a second honeymoon in Africa where the Duchess showed her prowess with a rifle. She has always been a good shot as Churchill knew when he presented her with a gun, soon after war broke out in 1939, with which to defend herself in an emergency. During the African travels Elizabeth 'proved herself a hardy campaigner and a lightening quick-change artist', according to Lady Asquith.

The following summer, spent as usual at Glamis and Balmoral, the Duchess knew she was pregnant. Her baby who would one day be Queen Elizabeth II, was delivered by Caesarean section at the Strathmore home in Bruton Street. Buckingham Palace announced: 'Her Royal Highness, the Duchess of York, was safely delivered of a Princess at 2.40 am this morning, April 21st'. But the rejoicing for a third heir to the throne was muted because of the imminent national industrial crisis. Eleven days later a general strike was called.

Crowds waited outside 17 Bruton Street in drizzling rain to watch the Home Secretary Sir William Joynson-Hicks arrive for the birth. It was still the custom that a home secretary must be present to ensure that an heir to the throne was truly the child of its parents and not a substitute. Elizabeth must have hated being monitored in this way and, significantly, she was the last royal mother to suffer the indignity. When Prince Charles – and later his children – were born, the custom was waived.

Both the King and the Duke of York were greatly concerned with the general strike. But it was decided that the baby's christening should proceed as normal. She was named Elizabeth, after her mother, Alexandra, after her great-grandmother who had died the year before, and Mary after her grandmother, in the chapel at Buckingham Palace. In her diary that evening, Queen Mary wrote: 'Of course poor baby cried'.

On 6 January 1927, a tearful Elizabeth said goodbye to her nine months' old daughter for a six-months' separation, for the Yorks were to tour Australia and New Zealand.

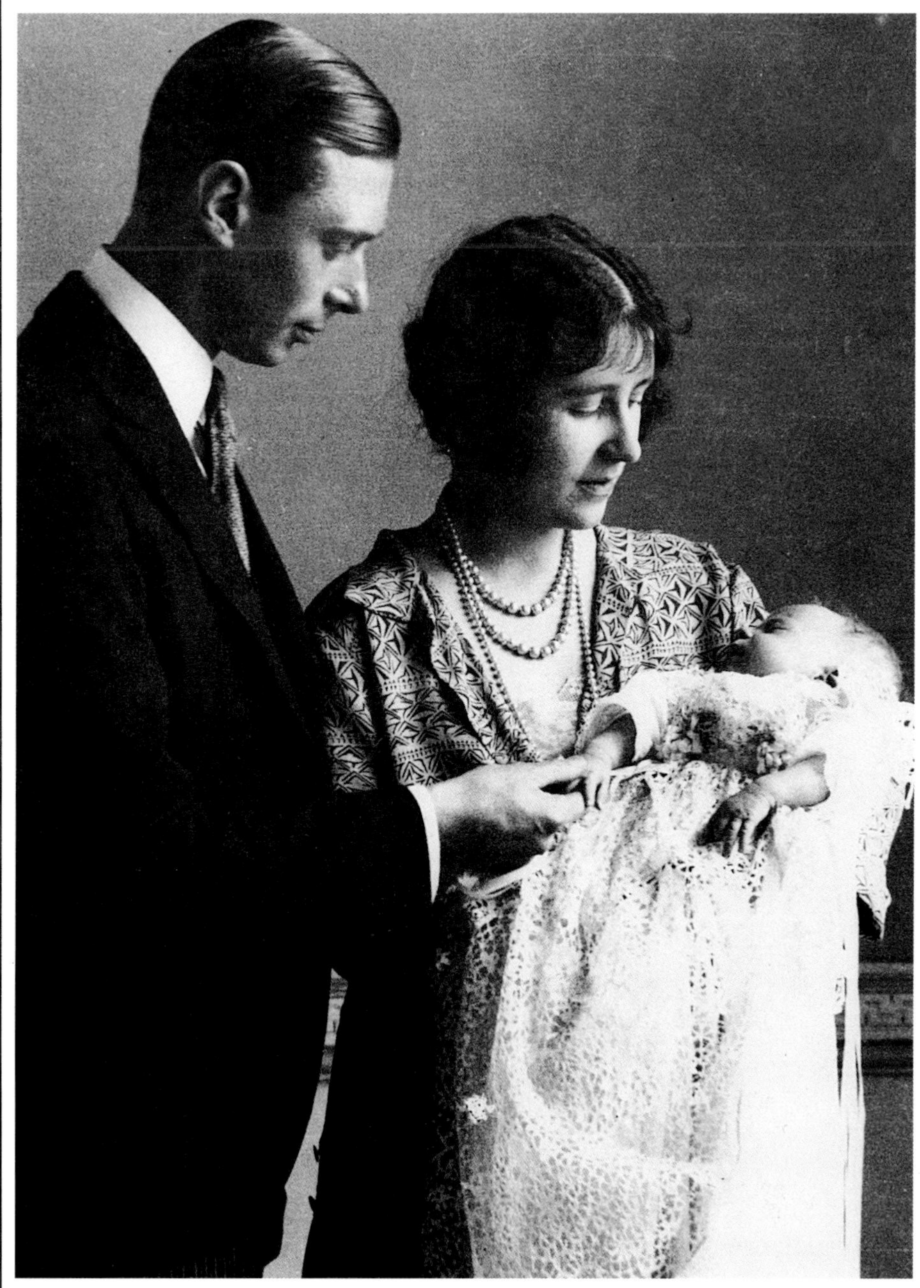

The Duchess of York holds her first-born. The baby daughter, named Elizabeth after her mother, was born on 21 April 1926.

The Duchess hugged her baby, struggling to hold back the tears, as the child stretched out to grab one of her father's shining uniform buttons, almost as if she was trying to hold him back. 'It quite broke me up', wrote Elizabeth to her mother-in-law later. At the time their car had to circle the adjoining square several times for her to regain her composure before the official public farewells.

During the highly successful tour, the Duchess met again several old friends who had convalesced at Glamis during the war.

The Duke and Duchess of York in Australia in 1927. They had to leave their daughter Elizabeth, who was eight months old at the time, in England. 'It quite broke me up' wrote the Duchess in a letter to her mother-in-law Queen Mary.

When she returned to Britain Elizabeth found her baby daughter contented and happy in the charge of 'Allah' who had once looked after the Bowes Lyon children. The Duchess followed her mother's example of being available as much as possible during her children's childhood. Nursery doors were never closed and 'Lilibet' – as she called herself – grew up with 'the sun always shining' as she would one day speak of her childhood.

Four years later, at Glamis – because August meant Scotland to the Duchess whether a baby was expected or not – her second daughter, Princess Margaret Rose, was born. She was the first royal child of any importance to be born north of the border for over 300 years and a huge bonfire was lit on a hill near the castle to celebrate the following day. Once again the birth, on 21 August 1930, was by Caesarean section, and, as was becoming usual for all the important events of the Duchess's life, it was raining. 'Our weather!', she said, looking down at her new daughter, as a thunderstorm raged above the castle.

Four months later, in November, as she began buying Christmas presents for her young family, Elizabeth's brother-in-law David, the Prince of Wales, was introduced to Mrs Wallis Simpson. It was an event which would eventually shatter the happy tenor of the York's life.

[1] Sir Henry 'Chips' Channon was an American who married Lady Honor Guinness and became an MP.

CHAPTER 4
QUEEN EMPRESS

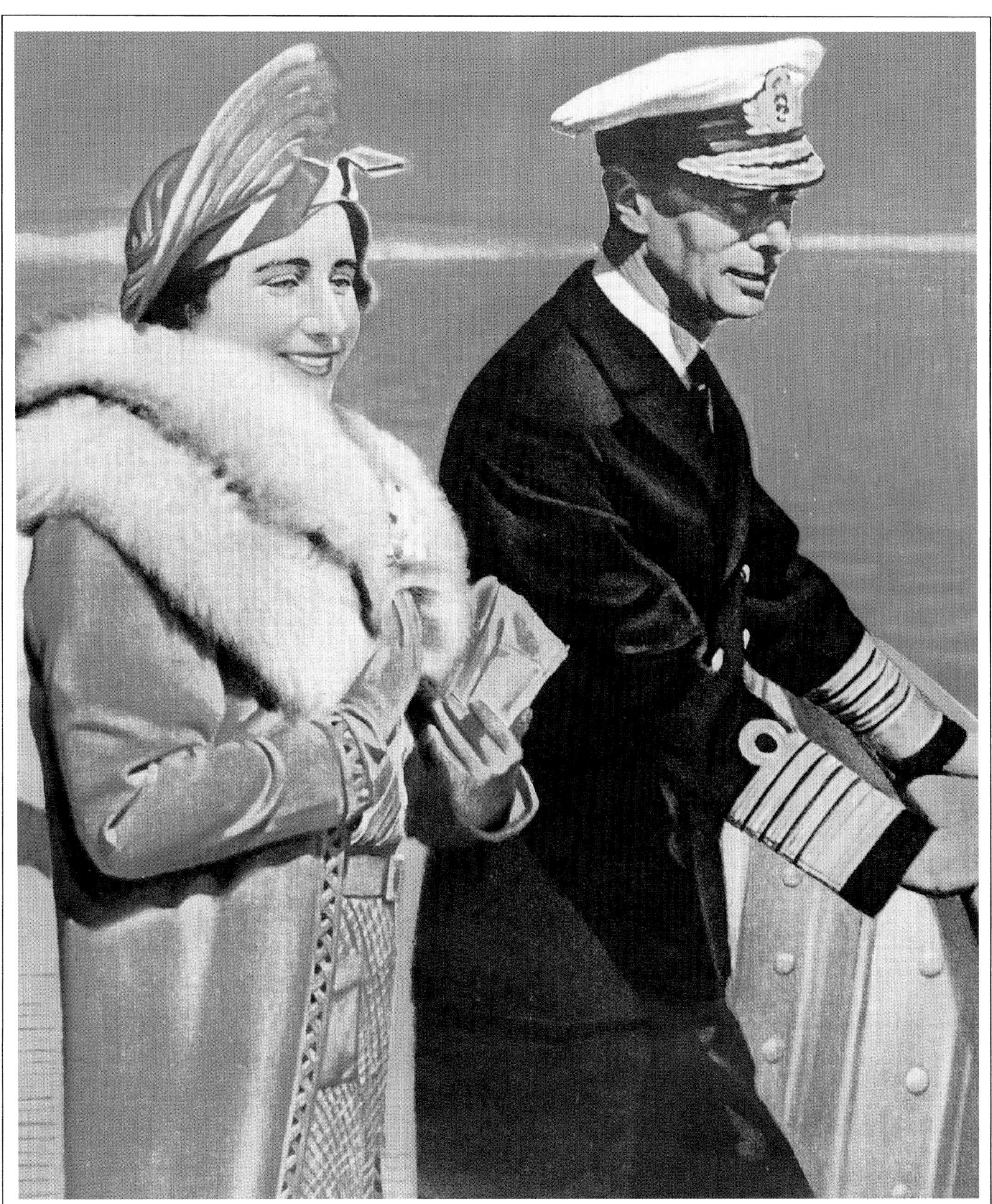

The sailor King and his Queen return from the United States and Canada to be greeted by enthusiastic crowds.

CHAPTER 4

QUEEN EMPRESS

THE 1930s which opened with unemployment reaching a peak of two million, proved a momentous and dramatic decade for Elizabeth and Bertie. They began it as Duke and Duchess of York and finished it, reluctantly and unexpectedly, as King and Queen.

As industrial problems mounted and the drums of war began to beat over Europe, their personal lives were shattered by the willow-slim, dark-haired Wallis Simpson from Baltimore, USA. 'She just blew in', Elizabeth said, 'and I wish she'd blow right out again'. When George V heard of the latest woman in the life of the heir to the throne he commented to Stanley Baldwin: 'After I am dead the boy will ruin himself in twelve months'.

It was a prophetic statement, but there were several years of being a sovereign and a grandfather before that day came. The King adored his 'sweet little Lilibet' and became increasingly fond of her mother – even though she got her way in the matter of her second daughter's name. Ann had been their original choice but the King had vetoed it. For the second choice Margaret – and Rose after her elder sister – Elizabeth did not consult

continued on page 57

Elizabeth was greatly influenced by her mother, the Countess of Strathmore. She was a woman of many accomplishments including gardening, painting, music and needlework. Above all she was a marvellous home-maker.

An oil painting by de Laszlo of the Duchess in a bare-shouldered, Edwardian-style gown

THE GOLDEN YEARS

Holding a business-like pair of binoculars to study form at Badminton in 1982.

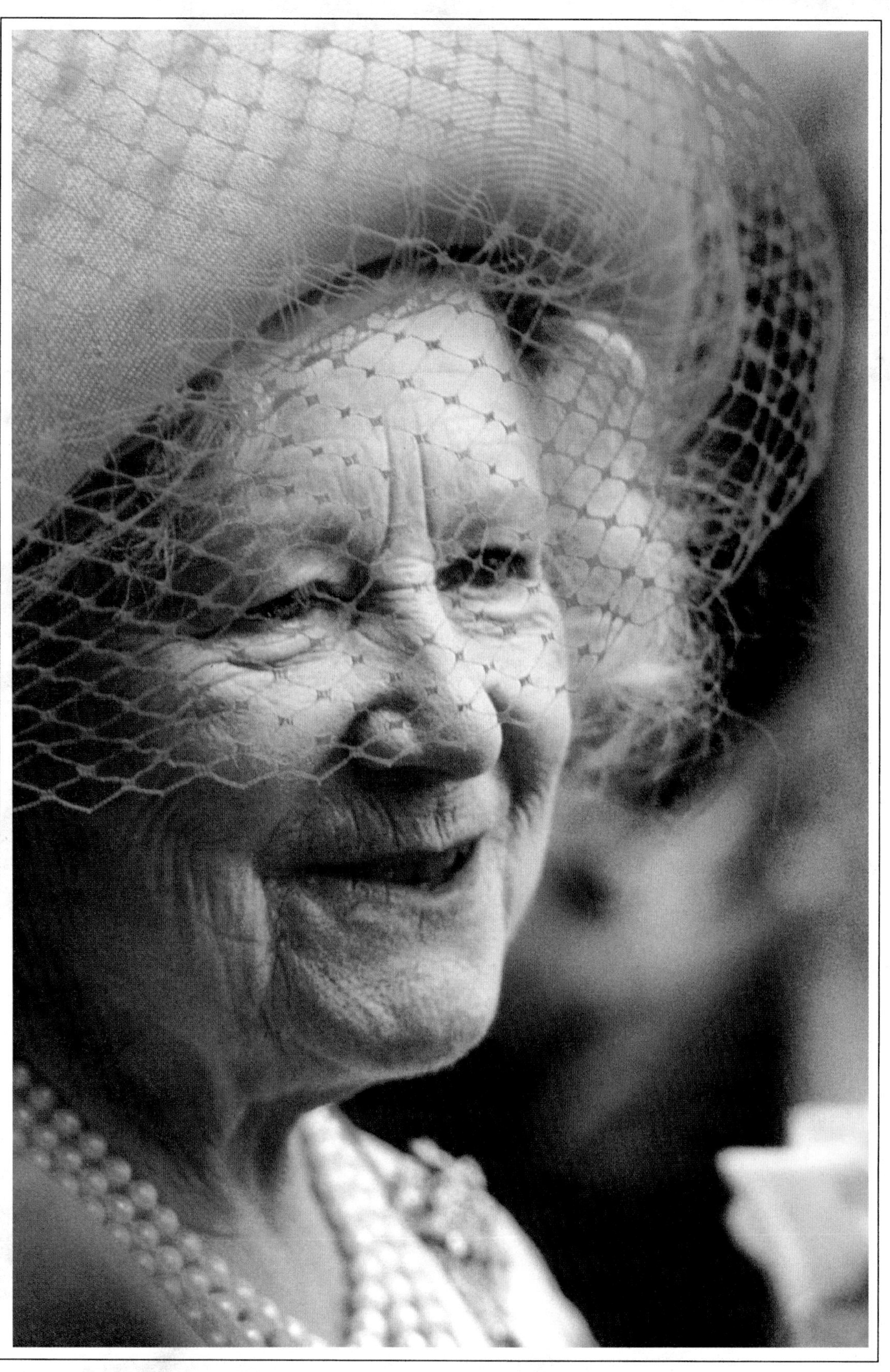

The Queen Mother always tried to attend local events at Sandringham. Here she admires the blooms at the Flower Show in 1985.

The Queen Mother meets the cast at the première *of the film* Room With a View.

ABOVE: *Pink roses for the 'Queen Mum' from a young admirer on her eighty-eighth birthday.*

RIGHT: *Resplendent in yellow for a visit to Keogh Barracks in June 1987.*

FAR RIGHT: *Two pairs of hands from two very different worlds: the Queen Mother meets another senior citizen at RAF Scampton in 1989.*

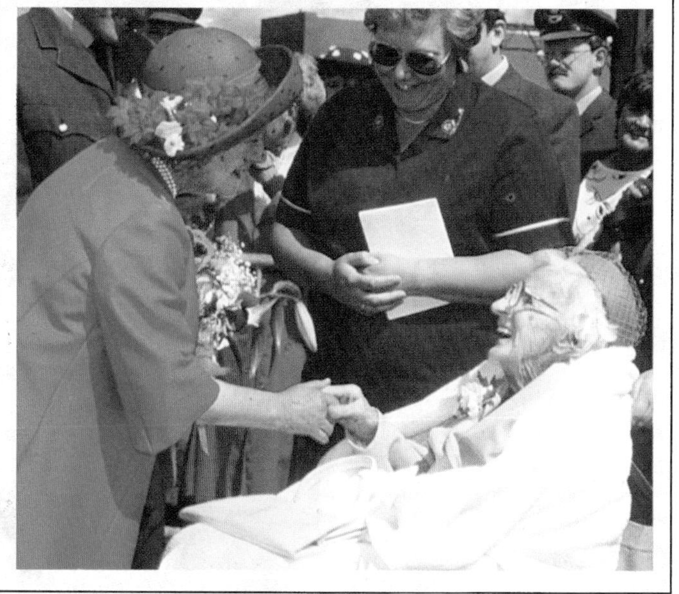

Here she may be in her eighties but the Queen Mother still loved an evening out. She wears a diamond tiara and a glamorous pink and blue organdie gown to a film première in 1989.

OVERLEAF LEFT AND RIGHT: *The now familiar appearance on her birthday, this time her eighty-ninth, outside Clarence House where the large crowd sang 'Happy Birthday'.*

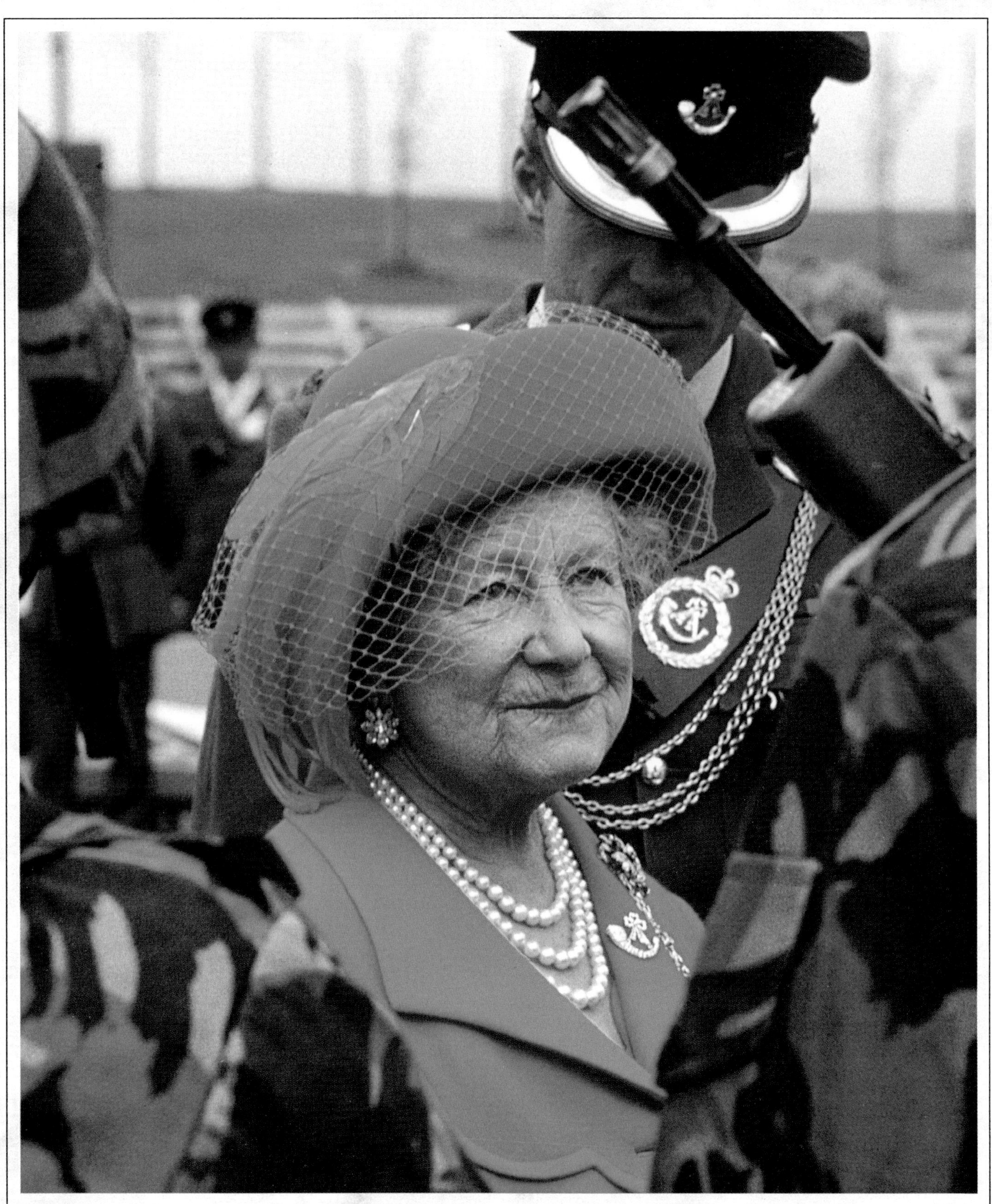

In her capacity as Colonel in Chief of the Light Infantry the Queen Mother inspects a guard of honour at Flowerdown, near Winchester.

continued from page 47

her in-laws but instead wrote to Queen Mary: 'Bertie and I have decided now to call our little daughter Margaret Rose . . . I hope you like it'.

Despite the distress and immense responsibility the decade was to bring them, it was a time of personal fulfilment and happiness. Their family life was greatly enhanced by a new country home, Royal Lodge, the pink-washed house in Windsor Great Park that came to mean so much to them.

It was at this time that the first of a long line of family corgis and a young Scots governess called Marion Crawford, who soon became known as 'Crawfie', came into their lives. She became famous not only for educating a future monarch in her most formative years, but because she 'spilt the beans' about it all.

This disloyalty incurred extreme regal displeasure but, in fact, Crawfie did the Royal Family a great service, revealing for posterity the intimate, but not intrusive, details of a very happy home. She also, in her own way, paid tribute to the Duchess – a mother of as outstanding a calibre as Lady Strathmore.

From Crawfie we learn of her first meeting with the Duchess of York:

> She had a sort of sheen or brightness about her in those days. She was thirty-one and her way of speaking was the easy, friendly one of any girl in her own home speaking to another girl who was far from home and might be a little homesick and needed to be put at her ease. She wore, as usual, blue and I still thought her one of the loveliest people I had ever seen. She had a gentle, kindly manner of looking at you. Her eyes were her most outstanding feature, very blue, very sympathetic and she looked incredibly youthful.

Crawfie described the 'wonderful atmosphere' of 145 Piccadilly, then the York's town house. 'It was a quiet and home-like life, the children seeing a great deal more of their parents than most London society children do . . .' The Duke and Duchess were 'so young and so much in love. They took great delight in each other and in their children'.

In the world outside 145 Piccadilly, child actress Shirley Temple was the darling of the cinema screens, Adolf Hitler became Head of State and Chancellor of Germany and the golden-haired Prince of Wales scintillated in an adoring Society circle which had now been joined by Wallis Simpson.

Thelma, Lady Furness had been the lover of the Prince before Mrs Simpson's arrival. By all accounts the Duchess of York got on well with her and Thelma liked Elizabeth. This inspired the fanciful thought that if she ever lived in a bungalow 'this is the woman I would most like to have as a next-door neighbour to gossip to while hanging out the washing in our backyards'. It was echoed most sincerely by a more down-to-earth voice years later when a cleaner at Sandringham told the Queen Mother over a cup of tea at the local Women's Institute: 'I should like to have you as a neighbour, Ma'am'.

In 1934, the Duchess of York acquired a sister-in-law: Marina, the tall, good-looking Greek Princess who married the youngest royal brother, George, Duke of Kent. But Elizabeth was closer to her other sister-in-law, Alice, the daughter of the 7th Duke of Buccleuch, who came from much the same aristocratic Scottish background as herself. She married Henry, Duke of Gloucester in 1935.

The same year King George V had celebrated his Silver Jubilee with a Thanksgiving Service at St Paul's Cathedral in London. Chips Channon described the York family driving through the City streets, 'the two tiny pink children waving more energetically than their parents'.

After the Jubilee the King's health sharply deteriorated. Increasingly fragile, he viewed uneasily the goings-on of his heir David and, eventually, voiced the thoughts he must have been stifling for years: 'I pray to God my eldest son will never marry and have children and that nothing will come between Bertie and Lilibet and the throne'. It is unlikely that his daughter-in-law heard this mentioned at the time but, with her perception, she must have been aware that over their heads there hung the shadow of a metaphorical crown. No observant onlooker within the Court circle could have missed the implications inherent in the Prince of Wales's apparent disregard for his responsibilities.

The Duchess did everything she could to make the King's last days happy. Lilibet had a bucket-and-spade holiday with him at Bognor and she herself saw him frequently, often seeking advice – something his own children rarely did. They both had a sense of humour that appealed to the other and spent many happy times together. When he died on 20 January 1936, Elizabeth was unwell herself, suffering from complications after 'flu. To the King's doctor Lord Dawson, she wrote: 'I miss him dreadfully. Unlike his own children I was never afraid of him and in all the twelve years of having me as a daughter-in-law he never spoke one unkind or abrupt word to me and was always ready to listen and give advice on one's silly little affairs. He was so kind and dependable and, when he was in the mood, he could be deliciously funny too'. An affectionate insight into George V's character and, surely, a revealing glimpse of Elizabeth too.

As 1936 mellowed into autumn so the new King Edward VIII's love for Wallis Simpson deepened. In

King George VI and Queen Elizabeth.

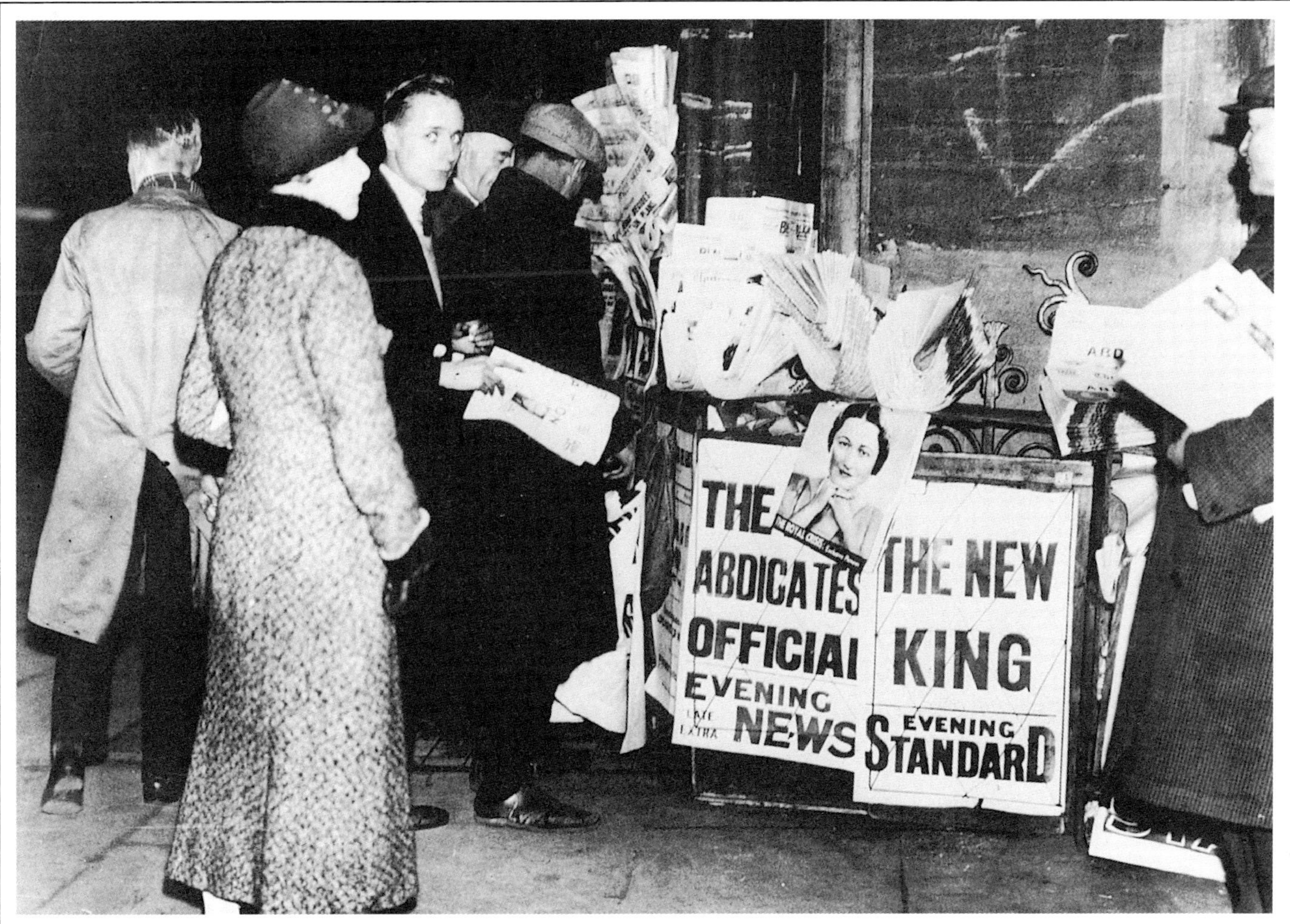

November he told the Prime Minister Stanley Baldwin that he wished to marry the American divorcee. The country was soon to be plunged into crisis.

The story of the abdication of King Edward VIII has been well documented. From Elizabeth's point of view the issues were clear cut. As a happily married wife and mother – and a deeply religious woman – she could not condone the new King's wish to marry a woman divorced from two husbands. Duty had been one of the strongest lessons of her childhood and her years as a royal Duchess had provided the consolidation. As wife of the heir to the throne and mother of the heiress presumptive, it held even more potency as a life's objective. But she did not want to be Queen. Nor did she wish to see Bertie or Lilibet assume the responsibility of monarchy. From the Duchess's correspondence with Lord Dawson we glimpse a little of her feelings:

> I am only suffering, I think, from the effects of a family break-up which always happens when the head of the family goes. Outwardly one's life goes on the same, yet everything is different, especially mentally and spiritually. I don't know whether it is the result of being ill but I mind things that I don't like more than before.

As if to further aggravate the situation her husband's stammer, until then considerably better, had returned. He called it 'God's curse upon me', and grew daily more edgy and nervous.

Elizabeth still felt wretched but determined to overcome it. As she put it: 'It will be very good for me to pull myself together and try to collect a little will-power'. But, uncharacteristically, she took to her bed again, as the crisis heightened, with a further bout of flu. It was something that tended to happen to her repeatedly when a situation was fraught – almost as if nerves and a sense of premonition precipitated an illness. To her four-poster bed in 145 Piccadilly, like a restless tide, came the daily news from Fort Belvedere to where the King had retreated. 'It is like sitting on the edge of a volcano', said

'We must take what is coming and make the best of it', said Elizabeth on the day she and her husband became King and Queen.

The two Elizabeths. Mother and daughter in Scotland when the young Princess was seven years old.

Elizabeth to her husband and mother-in-law who visited her frequently.

As the abdication crisis eddied around them the Duke found himself curiously isolated from the deliberations of the King and the government. He, who would be most affected by his brother's decision, was the last person consulted – something that rankles with the Queen Mother to this day. On 3 December 1936, Bertie wrote in his diary: 'David said to Mama that he could not live alone as King and must marry Mrs S . . .'

Alice, Duchess of Gloucester, tells in her memoirs of that meeting when she was staying with Queen Mary at Marlborough House. 'The King suddenly appeared after dinner. There were just the Queen, the Princess Royal and myself there at the time. He was in a great state of agitation and asked his mother if I could leave the room as he had a very serious family matter to discuss . . . it was not difficult to guess what it might be'.

Elizabeth, meanwhile, was still ill in bed and had to cope, moreover, with an extremely troubled husband who – as he put it himself – 'broke down and sobbed like a child' during a visit to Queen Mary. He had assessed what lay before him in a letter to Sir Godfrey Thomas, his brother's assistant private secretary: 'If the worst happens and I have to take over, you can be assured that I will do my best to clear up the inevitable mess, if the whole fabric does not crumble under the shock and strain of it all'.

Queen Mary, desperately upset herself, maintained a dignified composure throughout and was a stalwart support to her daughter-in-law. She comforted Elizabeth 'whose tears were streaming down her face', as Queen Mary noted in her diary. Marion Crawford saw the dowager Queen leave. 'She who was always so upright, so alert, looked suddenly old and tired. The Duchess was lying in bed, propped up among pillows. She held out her hand to me. 'I'm afraid there are going to be great changes in our lives Crawfie', she said. 'We must take what is coming to us and make the best of it'. Her storm of weeping over, the woman who would be the new Queen grew philosophic and calm. In the biggest crisis of her husband's life she would stoically sustain and support him through it all. If some steel entered her heart at this point which made her impervious to the feelings of her brother-in-law, now the Duke of Windsor, it is not so surprising.

The Windsor dynasty, splintered by the abdication, had to be stabilized. There could be no competition between the romantic figure of the exiled ex-King and his more diffident successor. Deeply protective and stoutly backed by Queen Mary, Elizabeth advocated that David stay away from Britain – a policy with which the King agreed totally. Permanent exile was assured by not according his future wife the title of 'Her Royal Higness' which would have obliged both Queen Elizabeth and Queen Mary to receive her should she visit Britain. They would have felt it necessary to offer courtesy to the royal title if not the holder. Sir Walter Monkton, the Duke of Windsor's advisor, saw the new Queen's point: 'Naturally she thought that she must be on her guard because the Duke of Windsor is an attractive vital creature who could become a rallying point for a subversive pro-Windsor party'.

As Queen Consort and first lady in the land, Elizabeth's influence at this time was decisive. She herself became the pivot upon which her small family unit an 'absolutely united circle' as the late Princess Alice, Countess of Athlone described them – rallied the rest of the Royal Family to present a united front. The Queen was right to be firm and fiercely protective. Lady Airlie remembered a conversation with Stanley Baldwin who thought King George VI would have a great deal to contend with: 'there's a lot of prejudice against him. He's had no chance to capture the popular imagination as his brother did. I'm afraid he won't find it easy going for the first year or two'. Lady Airlie replied that King George V had said to her: 'Bertie has more guts than the rest of his brothers put together'. In her opinion, Lady Airlie added, the King had excellent judgement.

And so it proved. The King and Queen felt insecure for the first few months but with his 'wife and helpmeet' by his side, George VI met the challenge, not only of kingship but of the Second World War when his leadership qualities inspired both loyalty and devotion.

Not only were there weighty matters of State to settle, Elizabeth had to move her family from the friendly, contented atmosphere of 145 Piccadilly to the regal formality of Buckingham Palace, with as little upset to the children as could be contrived.

Lady Airlie, as an old friend, was one of the first to be invited informally. She spotted the change in Buck

The Duchess of York receives posies from twins at a garden party in aid of the National Council for Maternity and Child Welfare at St James' Palace in 1935.

House, as the family call it, immediately. 'I saw that the room was already beginning to show traces of her own personality', she wrote after she went to tea with the Queen in her private sitting-room. 'The little feminine touches, which I have always associated with her. "It looks homelike already", I said spontaneously. The King smiled proudly . . . "Elizabeth could make a home anywhere", he said'.

Windsor, as Lady Diana Cooper noted on a weekend visit, was a more difficult task. Her bedroom with an adjoining bathroom, circa 1856, was 'throttlingly stuffy'. She and her husband had been close friends of the now Duke of Windsor and feared there might be a 'black list' of names who would not be welcome at the new Court. But after dinner Duff Cooper was invited by the Queen to her sitting-room where they had a long talk which lasted until after midnight. His wife, who had retired to their suite, commented: 'It's d'Artagnon (no! Buckingham); it's Bothwell; it's Potemkin; it's Lancelot; it's boring!' But whatever his wife's feelings, Queen Elizabeth had made another conquest – and a useful one – of an influential politician, later 1st Viscount Norwich. Afterwards, contrasting the new Court with the old at Fort Belvedere, Lady Diana said: 'That was an operetta, this is an institution'.

As she settled into her new role the Queen was concerned that not only would she look the part but that her appearance would help to promote all that was best in British materials and fashion. As a child she had always enjoyed dressing-up. Now she saw that her 'props' as she called them, could be used to enhance and publicize her role.

The King showed great interest in her clothes and an unexpected sense of theatre. He took couturier Norman Hartnell aside to show him the Winterhalter portraits at Buckingham Palace. 'His Majesty made it clear in his quiet way that I should attempt to capture this picturesque grace in the dresses I was to design for the Queen', recalled Hartnell. 'Thus it is to the King and Winterhalter that are owed the fine praises I later received for the regal renaissance of the romantic crinoline!.

The dresses he designed for Queen Elizabeth, captured in the photographs of Cecil Beaton, drew compliments from all over the world – glorious, imaginative, escapist ball gowns which set the scene for the next stage in Elizabeth's life: her crowning as Queen and last Empress of India.

For both the King and Queen their coronation on 12 May 1937, had a religious, almost mystical significance. The Archbishop of Canterbury, Dr Cosmo Lang, noticed the evening before the ceremony, after he had given them a blessing, there were tears in both their eyes. 'From that

The coronation of King George VI and Queen Elizabeth. In the royal box above are (from left to right): the Earl and Countess of Strathmore; the Duchess of Kent; the Duchess of Gloucester; Queen Maude of Norway; Queen Mary; Princess Elizabeth and Princess Margaret Rose; the Princess Royal.

LEFT: *The moment of crowning. 'It was an unforgettable experience', Queen Elizabeth said later.*

OPPOSITE: *Londoners prepare for the coronation in May 1937.*

moment I knew what would be in their hearts when they came to the anointing and crowning'. But before the majesty and symbolism of the 1,000-year-old ceremony absorbed them there were the less emotive moments to get through. Like being awakened after a short, restless sleep at 3.00 am, not only by loud-speakers being tested, but by the shouting and singing of the vast crowd camped outside the Palace. 'Sleep was impossible', wrote the King in his diary. 'I could eat no breakfast and had a sinking feeling inside – the hours of waiting before leaving for Westminster Abbey were the most nerve-wracking'.

He and Queen Elizabeth had practised for hours with Mr Logue's breathing exercises so that he would not stumble over his words during the ceremony. Each step they took in the Abbey had been rehearsed over and over again. Now they were the stars of a glittering, age-old ceremony and both rose superbly to the occasion.

Unfortunately the vast gold coronation coach had not been overhauled since George V's coronation and its unsteady motion made both the King and Queen feel ill. As they swayed and jolted along their discomfort was only eased by Elizabeth observing that, as usual, on all the great occasions of her life, it was raining. 'Queen's weather', smiled the King.

Queen Mary, who had broken with tradition to see her son crowned, made a deep curtsy from the royal box as her daughter-in-law, the new Queen, passed in her procession. Beside her the two Princesses, in lace frocks with silver bows and their first strings of pearls, curtsyed beautifully, as they had practised with their parents the night before.

For her coronation dress the Queen had gone not to Hartnell but, sentimentally and loyally, to Madame Handley-Seymour who had made her wedding dress. It was of ivory satin embroidered with the emblems of Britain and the Dominions in gold and diamanté. Her purple train flowed across the gold carpet of the Abbey making a ribbon of colour as her procession halted in the coronation amphitheatre.

As the Crown of St Edward, a replica of the original destroyed by Cromwell – first made with hired jewels for the Restoration coronation of Charles II and remade with

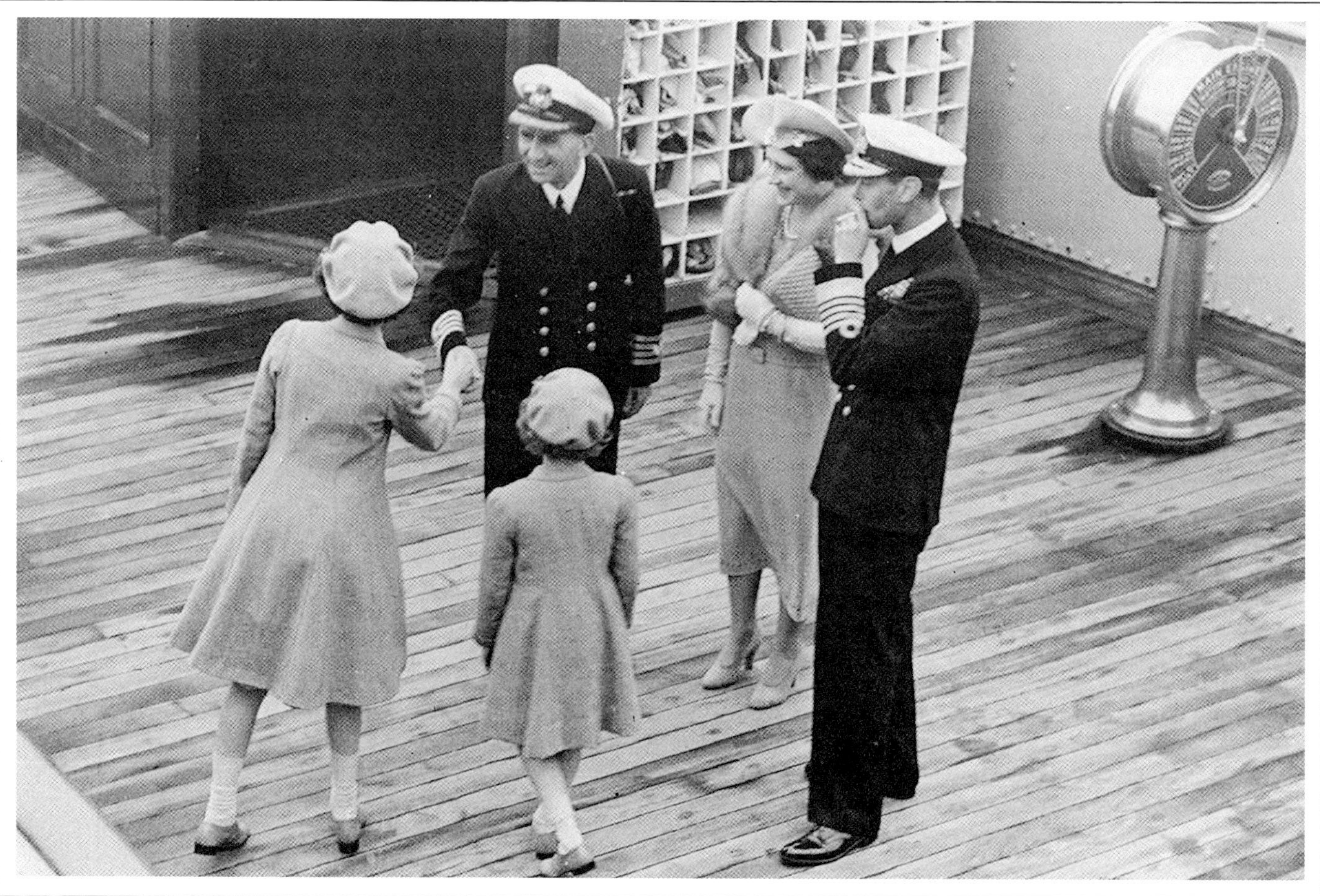

Home again after a great transatlantic success, the King and Queen are reunited with Princesses Elizabeth and Margaret Rose.

new stones for George V – was placed on her husband's head, Queen Elizabeth watched intently. Then came her own crowning when she was first anointed on the head with holy oil from the ampulla beneath a canopy of cloth of gold held by four duchesses. Her fourth finger received the ring and then the Archbishop placed the Consort's crown on her dark head. It had been especially made for her with, at its centre, the priceless and historic Koh-i-Noor diamond, said to bring ill luck to any male wearer. As Queen Mother, Queen Elizabeth wore the crown again at the coronation of her daughter Elizabeth II. At the moment of her crowning came the symbolic act her two young daughters had rehearsed over and over again. They put on their own slim golden coronets along with all the peeresses whose white-gloved arms rising upwards reminded Princess Elizabeth of swans.

Winston Churchill, his romanticism aroused by Edward VIII's love story, had supported the King before he abdicated. Now, as he watched Queen Elizabeth receiving the crown, he turned to Mrs Churchill and, his eyes full of tears, said: 'You were right; I see now "the other one" wouldn't have done'.

From her seat in the royal box next to the Duchess of Kent, Lady Strathmore watched her youngest daughter crowned Queen of Britain and the Dominions and Empress of India. Her heart, as she told her family later, was 'very full'. Queen Elizabeth was always to feel thankful that Lady Strathmore had been well enough to attend the coronation. For in June, the following year, with the King and Queen at her bedside, she died suddenly after a heart attack. It was just before a State visit to Paris and the Queen bravely decided to carry on with the arrangements, but postponing them until the following month. But the Court mourning that followed Lady Strathmore's death meant that the clothes in vivid summery colours designed by Hartnell for the visit, would no longer be suitable. 'Is not white a royal prerogative for mourning, Your Majesty?' he asked the King. An all-white

Despite the threat of war the King and Queen visited Canada and the United States in May 1939. They are pictured, wearing life-jackets, aboard the Empress of Australia *bound for Quebec.*

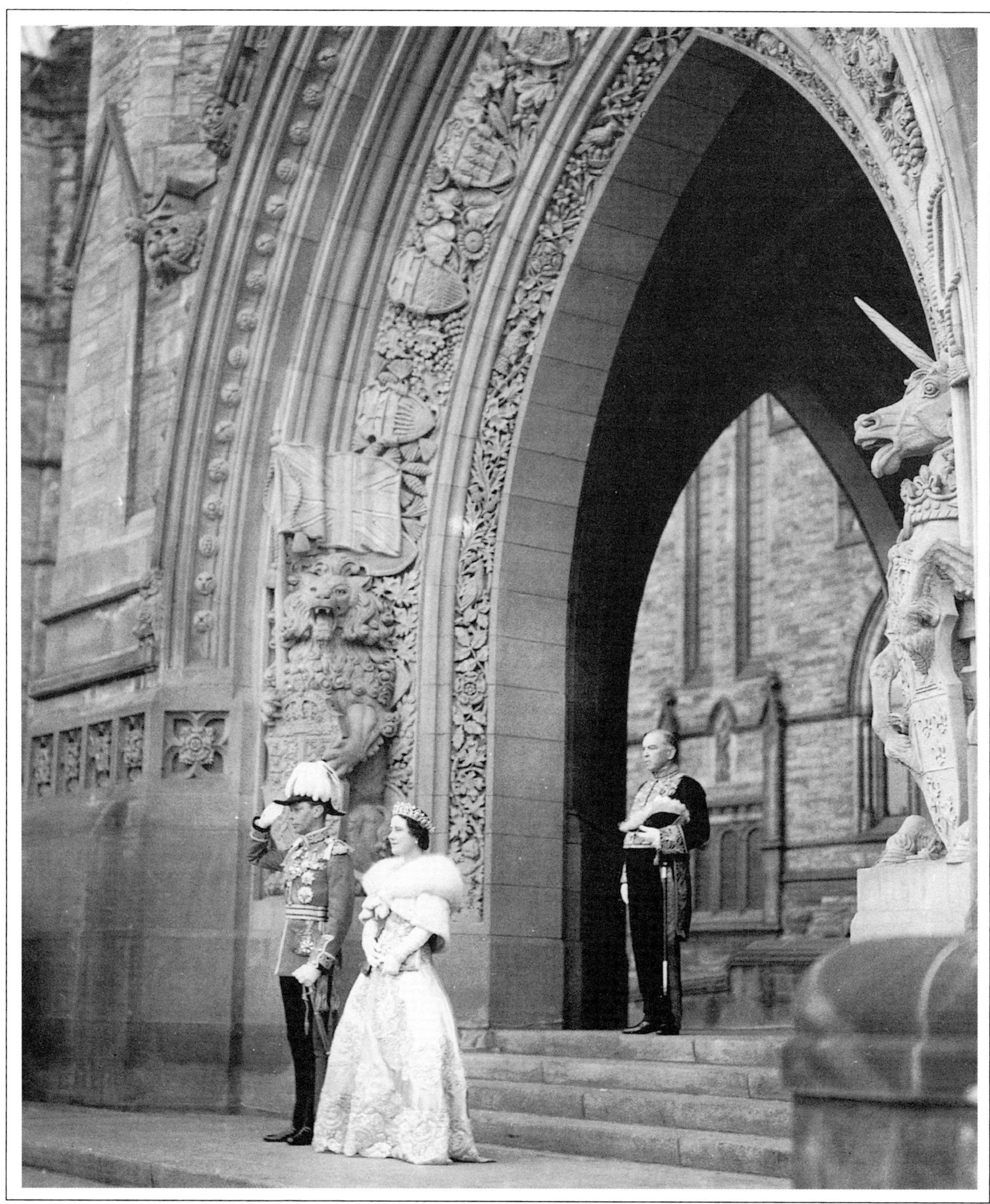

Outside the Houses of Parliament, Ottawa. For Queen Elizabeth it was the start of a love affair with Canada which has taken her back regularly over the years.

Visiting Niagara Falls before the King and Queen crossed over to the United States during the 1939 visit.

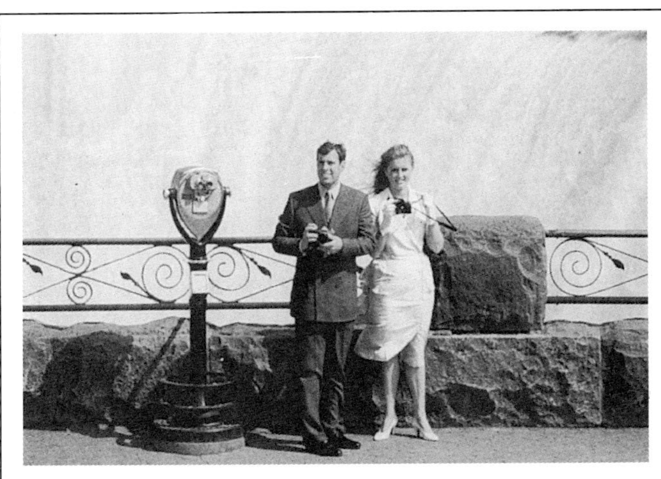

wardrobe was produced in two weeks with the Bruton Street salon working flat out, day and night. The clothes were delicate and ethereal and the chic Parisians were enchanted. 'We have taken the Queen to our hearts. She rules over two nations', wrote one French newspaper.

Adolf Hitler watching her success observed ruefully that Queen Elizabeth was 'the most dangerous woman in Europe'. He rightly sensed her charismatic power which would, one day, rally the nation's spirits at a time of great crisis. Three weeks before his troops had marched into Austria and, in October, would invade Czechoslovakia. The Nazi jackboots were on the move and pillage and ruin faced Europe. In April 1939 military conscription was introduced to Britain and plans for the evacuation of children from towns and cities were drawn up. The

LEFT: *Fifty years on the present Duke and Duchess of York enjoy the marvels of the 'Falls'.*

following month, despite the ominous war clouds, the King and Queen left for a visit to Canada and the United States. Trenches were being dug in London parks as they embarked on the liner *Empress of Australia* for Quebec where shouts of 'Vive le Roi' and 'Vive la Reine' greeted them. It was the first time a reigning British monarch had visited Canada and enormous crowds turned out to see them. Queen Elizabeth remembers them with affection and it was the start of a love affair with Canada which has taken her back regularly to that country. In July 1989, fifty years after that first visit, she sentimentally retraced a similar journey – but this time alone.

In America the King and Queen were also a tremendous success, making firm friends of President and Mrs Roosevelt and endearing themselves to the American people. It was a great public relations exercise on behalf of Britain poised on the brink of war and did much to advance Anglo-American relations.

Anne Morrow Lindbergh, pioneer woman flier and wife of the American aviator, described the Queen as 'like an old-fashioned rose, the small full ones, not brilliant in colour but very fragrant'. She noticed, also, the Queen's great talent which had developed naturally and always impressed those she met: '. . . she really looks at you, too, when she shakes hands. A real person looks out at you. How *can* she do it, when she goes through it so often?'

The trip to New York was part of a successful royal public relations exercise which did much to enhance Anglo-American relations.

In London, their huge transatlantic success had preceded them. Enthusiastic crowds waited to greet the royal couple, among them Sir Harold Nicolson who 'lost all dignity and yelled and yelled'. The Queen, he noted, was 'superb . . . in truth one of the most amazing Queens since Cleopatra'. Sir Harold also drew attention to the technique remarked upon by Anne Morrow Lindbergh which has since become so much a part of the Queen Mother's public image: 'She really does manage to convey to each individual in the crowd that he or she has had a personal greeting'.

They went up to Balmoral, as usual, for their summer holiday break only to be called back to London because of the impending crisis. 'Who is this Hitler spoiling everything?' asked Princess Margaret. Sirens wailed for the first time in London on 3 September 1939, and in Buckingham Palace the King wrote in his diary: 'Today we are at war again . . .' By his side the Queen was thinking of their daughters still in the Highlands with their governess. Princess Elizabeth was thirteen – just a year younger than the older Elizabeth had been on that August night in 1914 when she celebrated her birthday on the day the First World War broke out.

CHAPTER 5

WAR, PEACE AND A GRANDSON

The Queen Mother always loved hats – a passion she shared with granddaughter-in-law, the Princess of Wales. This one is decorated with ostrich feathers.

CHAPTER 5
WAR, PEACE AND A GRANDSON

HIS wife's belief and confidence in him and his own immense inner strength, wrought a great transformation in King George VI during the war years.

As a prelude to what turned out to be a dauntless performance for the remainder of his reign, the King decided he must speak 'live' to a nation facing unknown perils for the duration of the war. Again he and Elizabeth practised the breathing exercises which had so helped him in the past. The King never lost the nerves which attacked him relentlessly on these occasions. But, as usual, his wife found the right touch which made the 1939 Christmas broadcast so memorable. Always stirred by poetry, she drew the King's attention to lines by a retired university lecturer, Marie Louise Haskins, and on this inspirational note he finished his broadcast:

> I said to the man who stood at the Gate of the Year: 'Give me a light that I may tread safely into the unknown'. And he replied: 'Go out into the darkness and put your hand into the hand of God. That shall be unto you better than light and safer than a known way'.

After his death, Queen Elizabeth had the poem engraved on bronze plaques on the entrance to the King George VI Memorial Chapel at Windsor.

When the King was complimented on a speech, he would look at his wife and say: 'She helps me'. Queen Elizabeth, although she hated the sound of her own voice, and still does, discovered that she was a 'natural' broadcaster. Asking André Maurois, the French writer, to draft her a message for the women of France after the country fell to the Germans, she said: 'I want a human speech'. Maurois said afterwards: 'Now I have met Titania'.

'Britannia' would have been a more apt description. There was nothing imaginary or supernatural about the diminutive form that practised shooting in the gardens of Buckingham Palace where a target had been set up. As the pink walls of Royal Lodge were painted khaki for the duration, the Queen – expertly handling a .38 revolver, given to her by Winston Churchill, and a .303 rifle – said resolutely: 'They will not take me easily'. The King kept a sten gun beside him when they travelled by car. The chauffeur had instructions to drive on, if attacked, while the King defended them by shooting it out with the enemy. Both determined that if the worst happened they 'would not go down like the others' – an allusion to the European royalty who had fled into exile. 'If need be I will die here fighting', said the King. If that happened those close to them knew the Queen would be by his side.

Initially Queen Elizabeth felt that her contribution must include boosting morale by being seen as often as possible. She travelled the country in the bullet-proof royal train. Between them the King and Queen covered half a million miles in the train during the war. They visited evacuees, hospitals, civil defence units, Red Cross centres, bomb sites and service headquarters. The distressing visits to devastated areas became increasingly frequent as the Blitz got under way and, after each grim raid, the King and Queen could be seen picking their way through the debris – comforting and cheering folk as they went. Despite the hardship the Queen's still radiant smile and her soft, sympathetic voice made people feel less wretched. 'For him we had admiration. For her adoration', said one bomb victim. On a bomb site in the East End, a Cockney voice put it another way: 'Cor, ain't she luverley – ain't she just bloody luverley?'

At the outbreak of war the Queen was appointed Commander-in-Chief WRNS and Commander-in-Chief WAAF. But she never wore a uniform. 'Some clothes do

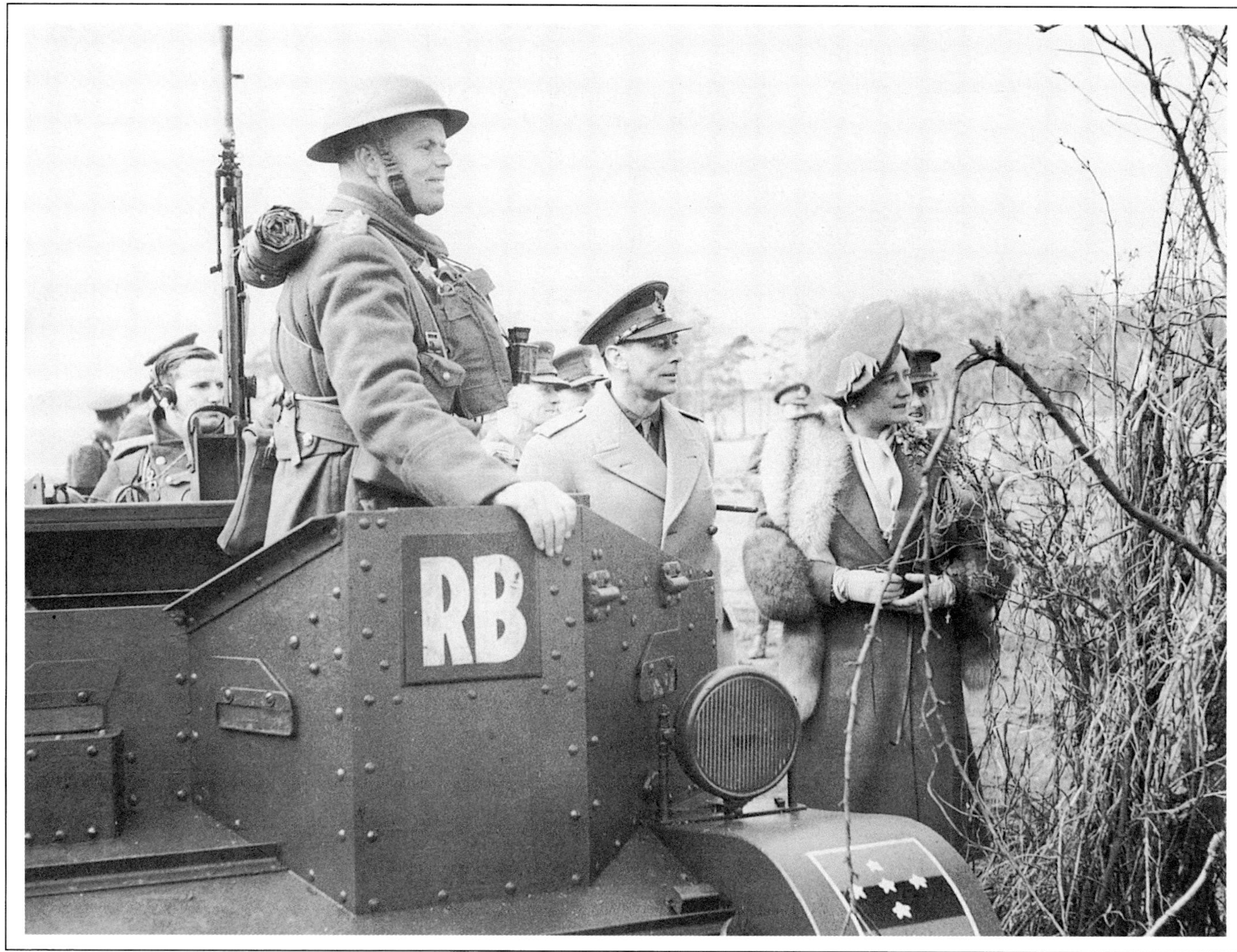

The King and Queen on one of their many wartime visits to the armed services.

not like me', she explained. And, besides, the King did not like her in anything unfeminine. 'Bertie likes to see me in fluffy frocks', she said once and never changed her style. Instead of uniform, Norman Hartnell – whom she persuaded to design attractive 'utility' clothes for 'every-woman' – made her outfits in dusty pink, blue and lilac which would 'convey the most comforting, encouraging and sympathetic note possible'. They were colours that also reacted kindly to the shattered and dusty areas in which she found herself, like the bombed building where a woman was weeping over a hole, under some wreckage, from which her terrified terrier refused to emerge. 'Let me try – I'm good with dogs', said the Queen who has indeed loved them all her life. Gentle coaxing brought the terrier out and the Queen found herself hugging an ecstatic but filthy Blitz survivor.

Her own dogs – at one count there were eight at Royal Lodge – were at Windsor with her daughters who spent the war behind the castle's protective stone walls. All the fine old paintings had been removed and the crystal chandeliers stored away. In the vaults under the castle, in leather hatboxes, wrapped up in old newspapers, were the Crown Jewels.

The King and Queen telephoned the children every night at 6 o'clock and each weekend they arrived in time for tea on Friday. Then, according to Marion Crawford, the Queen never showed she was worried. 'At that time she seemed to drop her cares at the gates of Royal Lodge and become just "Mummy" during her stay there'.

Rationing had been introduced in Britain in January 1940: four ounces of butter, twelve ounces of sugar and four ounces of bacon or ham for each person per week. In Buckingham Palace rations were strictly administered. When Winston Churchill, now Prime Minister, came for his top-secret 'briefing' luncheons with the King, he was served by the security-conscious Queen. 'I expect it is sawdust sandwiches again', joked her husband. Chef René Roussin did his best but Eleanor Roosevelt, wife of the American president reported, when she stayed there, that the food was no better than any wartime canteen – although served on gold and silver dishes.

On 13 May 1940, Queen Wilhelmina of the Netherlands arrived in exile, after her country had fallen to the Germans. She wore a tin hat and the clothes in which she had fled. Princess Alice of Gloucester recalls how Queen Wilhelmina could not join them for dinner that night because, as she was a large lady, there was nothing suitable in Buckingham Palace that would fit. 'There she was a forlorn little figure in little more than a mackintosh', wrote Princess Alice.

The next day the Queen got Hartnell round to deal with the situation. But the courageous Dutch Queen would not forsake her tin hat for any of the morale-boosting frivolities shown by the milliner who had come with Hartnell. Finally, 'that will do', she said pointing to a serviceable black hat worn by one of the assistants.

Queen Wilhelmina had seen her country invaded and her mood was understandable. Queen Elizabeth, albeit in a different position, had a rather contrasting attitude when visiting folk distressed by bombing or bereavement. 'Those poor people would wear their best if they came to see me. So I will wear my best for them', she once said.

As with the first war, Elizabeth's life was greatly saddened by Bowes Lyon family tragedy. Her nephew Patrick, the Master of Glamis, was killed on active service and another nephew, Andrew Elphinstone, was a prisoner of war, as was the King's nephew George Lascelles, son of the Princess Royal. Despite it all, as Mrs Clementine (later Lady) Churchill wrote in a letter to her daughter Mary, about a lunch at Buckingham Palace in 1941: 'The Queen is so gay and witty and very, very pretty close up'. On another occasion she wrote of spending more than an hour with Queen Elizabeth after dinner when the King and Mr Churchill were closeted together with post-prandial brandy and cigars. 'But it passed in a flash because she is gay and amusing and has pith and point'.

The Minister of Food, Lord Woolton, asked the Queen's permission to call helpers for a 'meals-on-wheels' emergency service, 'Queen's Messengers'. 'But why my title. What will I have done?' asked the Queen. Lord Woolton explained that the vast majority of people 'think of you as a person who would speak the kindly word and, if it fell within your power, would take the cup of hot soup to a needy person'. 'Do you really think I mean that?' said the Queen. 'It is what I have tried so very hard to be'.

In the spring of 1940, the Palace was rapidly filling up with royal refugees from Europe. On 27 May, Boulogne fell, cutting off the retreat of British troops. In Buckingham Palace the King and Queen waited as the armada of little ships achieved the miracle of Dunkirk and both knelt in prayer when they heard that the majority of the British Expeditionary Force had been rescued.

That summer, as the Battle of Britain began in the skies above London and southern England, it was suggested that the Princesses should be evacuated to Canada. To this the Queen replied: 'The Princesses would never leave without me and I couldn't leave without the King and the King will never leave'. To Sir Harold Nicolson the Queen added: 'I should die if I had to leave'.

On 18 August the first German plane was brought down over London and on 9 September Buckingham Palace itself was hit when a bomb fell on the north side shattering all the windows. The King and Queen were at Windsor but three days later they narrowly escaped death or serious injury when the Palace was again attacked. 'All

Queen Wilhelmina of the Netherlands sought refuge in Britain and then America after her country was invaded by the Germans.

Buckingham Palace was bombed in September 1940.

OPPOSITE: *The King and Queen comforting Blitz victims in 1940.*

of a sudden we heard an aircraft making zooming noises above us', wrote the King in his diary, 'saw two bombs falling past the opposite side of the Palace and then heard two resounding crashes as the bombs fell in the quadrangle about thirty yards away. We looked at each other and then we were out in the passage as fast as we could get there. The whole thing happened in a matter of seconds. We all wondered why we were not dead'. 'I am glad we have been bombed', said Queen Elizabeth. 'I feel I can look the East End in the face'.

It had clearly been a planned raid on the Palace and an attempt to kill the King and 'the most dangerous woman in Europe' as Hitler had once called the Queen. Writing later about the bombing Churchill revealed that he had no idea at the time 'of the peril of that particular incident. Had the windows been closed instead of open, the whole of the glass would have splintered into the faces of the King and Queen causing terrible injuries. So little did they make of it that even I, who saw them and their entourage so frequently, only realized long afterwards what had actually happened'.

After their narrow escape, the King and Queen went to inspect the damage and found their French chef René Roussin trying to cook luncheon in the debris of his kitchen. Despite the mess a delicious smell of roasting grouse came from the oven where Roussin was calmly basting the birds. His grimy face crinkled into a smile as the Queen said: 'Thank goodness the stove is working'. 'Good', said the King, 'I'm very hungry'.

On another occasion M Roussin recalled he was called to the Chinese Dining-Room as air raid sirens whined. The King and Queen were alone in the candlelight and the chef thought they might have felt lonely in the half-empty palace. 'They complimented me on my dinner', he remembered. 'And asked me to have a glass of wine with them. His Majesty poured it himself and the Queen raised her glass. In my own language she said: "To La Belle France and her brave fighters"'.

Another memory of the wartime Queen told to Lady Longford, was from an officer stationed at Windsor Castle: 'One evening she returned late from London after a dreadful day. Hundreds of houses down, streets up, people crying. The lot. But she came down to the Quadrangle to see us at the household dinner in the Star Chamber, as she always did, and laughed and joked with the children. And what she was like with the King! For ever loving and soothing . . .'

Worry of another kind came one day at Windsor when a deserter, unbalanced by the death of his family in an air raid, found his way to the Queen's room and grabbed her by the ankles. 'For a moment my heart stood still', she said later. But to the man she said quietly: 'Tell me about it'. The sad story was unfolded to an increasingly sympathetic Queen who told the King afterwards: 'Poor man – I felt so sorry for him'. When a similar incident befell her elder daughter in July 1982, the Queen Mother comforted her: 'I know, I've been through it too', she said.

In August 1942, the Royal Family went for a brief stay to Balmoral. They were sitting at dinner with the Duke and Duchess of Gloucester – now Princess Alice – when the King was called to the telephone. Princess Alice described how 'each one of us and particularly Queen Elizabeth suspecting something awful had happened. The King came back and sat in silence. I could feel he was in

deep distress'. Nothing was said until the time the ladies retired from the dining-room. But later, when the Queen went back to speak to her husband, he told her of the death of his brother the Duke of Kent: his plane had crashed into a Scottish mountain. The King took some solace from the fact that he had been on active service with the RAF at the time – it was yet another tragic consequence of the war.

America was not yet in the war when Mrs Eleanor Roosevelt, their old friend from the pre-war US visit, came to stay with the King and Queen to get a first-hand view of how Britain was bearing up under the war-time conditions. Her hostess gave up her own bedroom, 'an enormous room without any windows having glass', Mrs Roosevelt could not help noticing. It was heated by a one-bar electric stove and, used to central heating, she was permanently cold. The King had, himself, painted Plimsoll lines on the baths in the private apartments so that nobody would take too much water.

Victory in Europe day, 8 May 1945. The Royal Family with their wartime comrade Winston Churchill on the balcony of Buckingham Palace.

Mrs Roosevelt wrote later that 'Buckingham Palace is an enormous place and without heat. I do not see how they keep the dampness out!' Both the King and Queen had colds and Mrs Roosevelt soon got one too. The next day, after her arrival, the Queen took her guest round the blitzed East End and said: 'The only solace in the destruction was that new housing would replace the slums'.

Throughout the war the King fretted because he could not be with his fighting men. 'He feels so much at not being more in the firing line', wrote the Queen to Queen Mary. But, as the war progressed towards eventual victory, he was able to spend more time with his armed forces. Visiting the Eighth Army in North Africa, the King's plane was diverted because of thick fog near Gibraltar. The Queen, waiting for news of his safe arrival, went through an agonizing time until the news came. Any wartime flight was hazardous and 'of course I imagined every sort of horror', wrote Elizabeth to her mother-in-law Queen Mary, 'and walked up and down my room staring at the telephone'.

Princess Elizabeth was eighteen in 1944 and begged to join the ATS (Auxiliary Territorial Service). As Second Lieutenant Elizabeth Windsor she learnt to drive and maintain a car. 'We had sparking plugs all last night at dinner', commented the Queen dryly.

After D-Day on 6 June 1944, the King visited troops on the Normandy beaches. Later that summer, as the French led the allies into Paris, the Royal Family felt they needed a break at Balmoral. Among those invited was a young naval officer Prince Philip of Greece, a cousin of Marina, the Duchess of Kent. 'They have been in love for the last eighteen months', Queen Mary confided to Lady Airlie, 'but the King and Queen feel she is too young to be engaged yet.' Both her parents wanted Lilibet to see more of the world – and meet more suitable men – before she settled down. In the meantime, in the course of the next few years, Philip became a British citizen and took the name of Mountbatten.

OPPOSITE ABOVE: *Queen Elizabeth visited a communal feeding centre in 1946. One little chap was ready for action.*

OPPOSITE BELOW: *Talking to Commonwealth soldiers at the Union Jack Club during the war.*

The King and Queen welcomed in Durban during their 1947 visit to South Africa.

Royal engagement. Elizabeth and Philip looking radiantly happy in the grounds of Buckingham Palace.

That November Queen Elizabeth's father, the Earl of Strathmore, died. At Glamis she listened with tears in her eyes and a mind full of memories, as pipers played *The Flowers of the Forest* over his grave.

At last, in 1945, the war ended. Huge crowds at the Victory in Europe celebrations cheered the King and Queen who were standing on the Palace balcony. With them were the Princesses – Lilibet in uniform – who were later allowed to go out and mingle with the crowds, accompanied by young officers.

Three months later came the end of the war with Japan and more celebrations. Afterwards the King said he felt 'burnt out'. Queen Elizabeth, too, was suffering from a reaction and 'quite exhausted after seeing so much sadness, sorrow, heroism and magnificent spirit – they deserve a better world', she commented in a letter to Queen Mary.

In 1947, the King, Queen and Princesses paid a visit to South Africa – one of the happiest journeys of their lives and the last all four would make together. During the trip an old Afrikaner said to the Queen: 'We still feel sometimes that we can't forgive the English for conquering us'. 'I understand perfectly', said the Queen. 'We feel very much the same in Scotland'.

Princess Elizabeth had been unofficially engaged to Philip Mountbatten before the trip and when they

returned to Britain it was made official. Their wedding in Westminster Abbey on 20 November 1947, organized most beautifully by Queen Elizabeth, was an emotional day for her as memories of her marriage to Bertie in that same Abbey, came flooding back.

The wedding of the future Elizabeth II was, said Winston Churchill, 'a flash of colour on the hard road we have to travel'. 'A week of gaiety such as the court has not seen for years', observed Lady Airlie. The King wrote to his daughter: 'I have watched you grow up all these years with pride under the skilful direction of Mummy, who as you know, is the most marvellous person in the world in my eyes . . .'

The following April they celebrated their Silver Wedding and the Queen, in a silvery blue gown, said that she was 'deeply thankful for our twenty-five years of happiness together, for the opportunities we have been given of service to our beloved country and for the blessings of our home and children . . . Looking back over the last twenty-five years and to my own happy childhood I realise more and more the wonderful sense of security and happiness which comes from a loved home'.

But the days of that life together were growing shorter. The King still felt exhausted and now he began complaining of cramps in his legs which turned out to be a circulatory obstruction. Prince Charles was born to

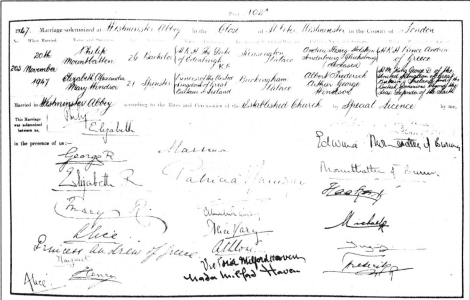

The Queen chats to her mentor Queen Mary as Elizabeth and Philip wave to the crowds on their wedding day. (Note the royal marriage certificate.)

The birth of a grandson. The Queen Mother has always thought that Prince Charles closely resembles his grandfather King George VI.

Elizabeth and Philip on 14 November 1948 and Queen Elizabeth found herself torn between happiness at the birth of a grandson and anxiety over the King's condition.

'I wish Allah could have seen him', she said to her sister, Lady Rose Granville. Their old nurse had died soon after the war ended; on her coffin was a wreath made entirely of violets – her favourite flower which they had once picked together in the Walden Bury Woods. A hand-written card read: 'In loving and thankful memory. Elizabeth R.'

After Prince Charles's christening, Queen Elizabeth got out the family photograph albums and they all tried to decide who the baby looked like. Queen Mary was quite definite: 'He looks like his great-great-great-grandfather Prince Albert', she said. Queen Elizabeth thought – and still does – that it was another Prince Albert, his grandfather, the King, that Prince Charles resembled.

CHAPTER 6
WIDOWHOOD

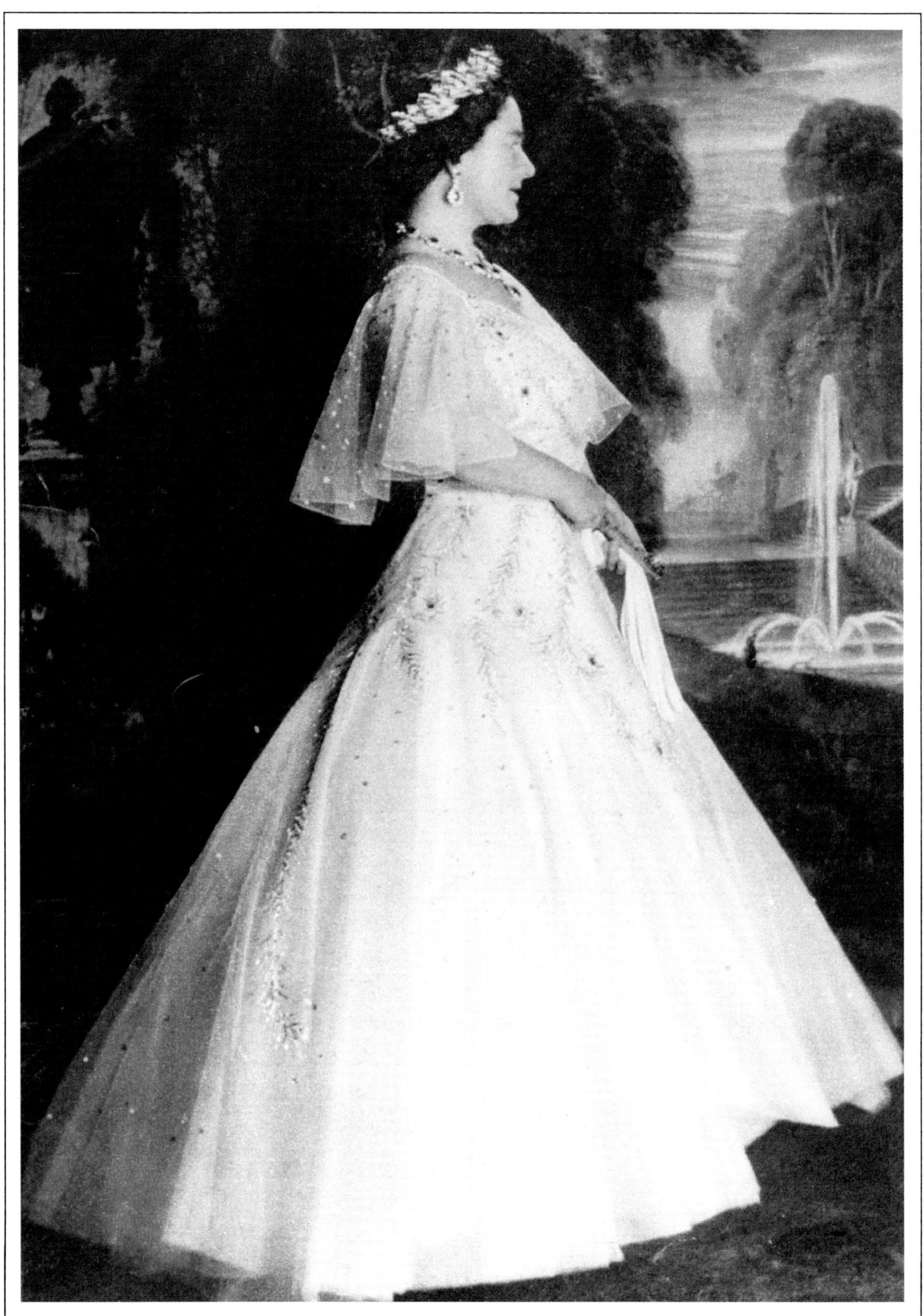

A Hartnell creation in crinoline, worn with the favourite ruby and diamond necklace.

OPPOSITE: *An armful of yellow roses for a Queen who loved flowers. She was always surrounded by flowers and requested that bouquets should not be wired so she could enjoy them in vases at home.*

CHAPTER 6
WIDOWHOOD

THE early years of the Fifties were for Queen Elizabeth, who was usually so happy and optimistic, a time when she was under considerable strain. Her husband was extremely ill. The cramps in his legs had been diagnosed as arteriosclerosis and there was, warned the doctors, a danger of gangrene. The fact had to be faced and, at the same time, concealed from a nation plunged into a post-war low after the exhilaration of victory. It was a tall order for any anxious wife but, as usual, Queen Elizabeth proved equal to it. Her smile did not falter and her charm was no less warm. But, all the time, gnawing away in her mind, was the spectre of the King's illness.

In the summer, at Balmoral, he still insisted on shooting and even devised an ingenious method of having himself pulled up hills by pony and harness with an emergency release in case the pony bolted.

The King was in the Highlands, as usual, in August, when the Queen phoned him from Clarence House where she was enjoying a glass of champagne with her son-in-law, the Duke of Edinburgh. Lilibet had a daughter, born on 15 August 1950, just before noon. They called her Anne – the name George V had vetoed for Princess Margaret and a favourite of the King and Queen. By the following May, the King developed what appeared to be complications after 'flu. Queen Elizabeth had gone alone to Ireland rather than postpone their visit and remembers how her heart sank when she telephoned to find her husband no better. 'Now they say there's something wrong with me blowers', he said. When she returned, the illness was found to be lung cancer and an immediate operation ordered. But the surgeons found it was too late and had to break the news to the Queen that her husband had only a short time to live. She kept the secret bravely although it must have taxed her unbearably.

On Prince Charles's third birthday, he and his grandfather were photographed together, a picture that Queen Elizabeth keeps by her side always. They all had Christmas at Sandringham but it was to be the King's last

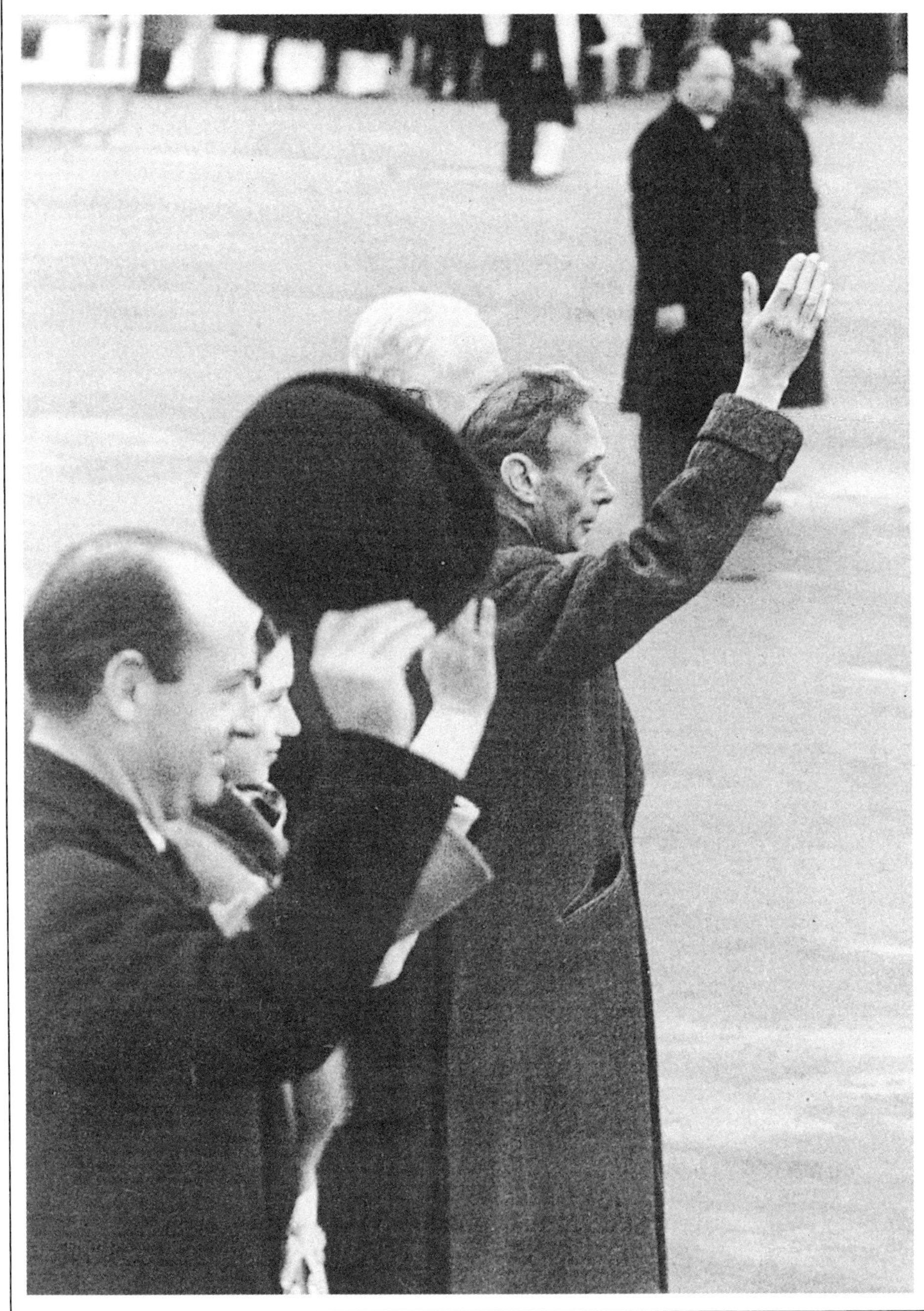

A last wave from her father as Princess Elizabeth sets off in his place on a Commonwealth tour. Already the King was gravely ill; within a week he would be dead.

festival with his family. On 29 January he told his wife he felt much better and they had a family farewell outing for Lilibet and Philip to see *South Pacific* at the Drury Lane Theatre. Next morning the King insisted on standing in a piercingly cold wind at London airport to wave goodbye to his eldest daughter and her husband, setting off on a Commonwealth tour in his place. By his side was his wife, apparently relaxed and smiling, although Princess Margaret looked pinched and worried. It was Queen Elizabeth's last public appearance with the King and, as always, she smiled her way through it – although her heart was heavy.

Behind them lay a happy Christmas holiday at Sandringham. The King did not have the agony of undertaking a 'live' broadcast to the nation which had always cast a shadow over previous Christmas Days. Instead, because of his health, he had spent weary hours recording it, sentence by sentence, because it was so difficult to speak more than a few words at a time. They saw the New Year in together in the old Scottish way and the Queen sang him the songs he had first heard when he was courting her at Glamis more than thirty years before.

On 5 February the King spent the day shooting. It was perfect Sandringham weather, 'blue sky, sunshine, and long shadows, a crispness underfoot and the call of mating partridges ringing clearly across broad fields', recalled his friend Aubrey Buxton who was a member of that last 'Keeper's Day' shooting party. The King shot nine hares and a pigeon and said to his estate workers, gamekeepers and friends: 'A good day's sport, gentlemen'.

Knowing he was happily occupied Queen Elizabeth and Princess Margaret went to visit painter Ted Seago who lived at nearby Ludham. They brought back some paintings for the King to see. Meanwhile he had twice walked over to the kennels to make sure a thorn had been removed from his golden retriever's paw.

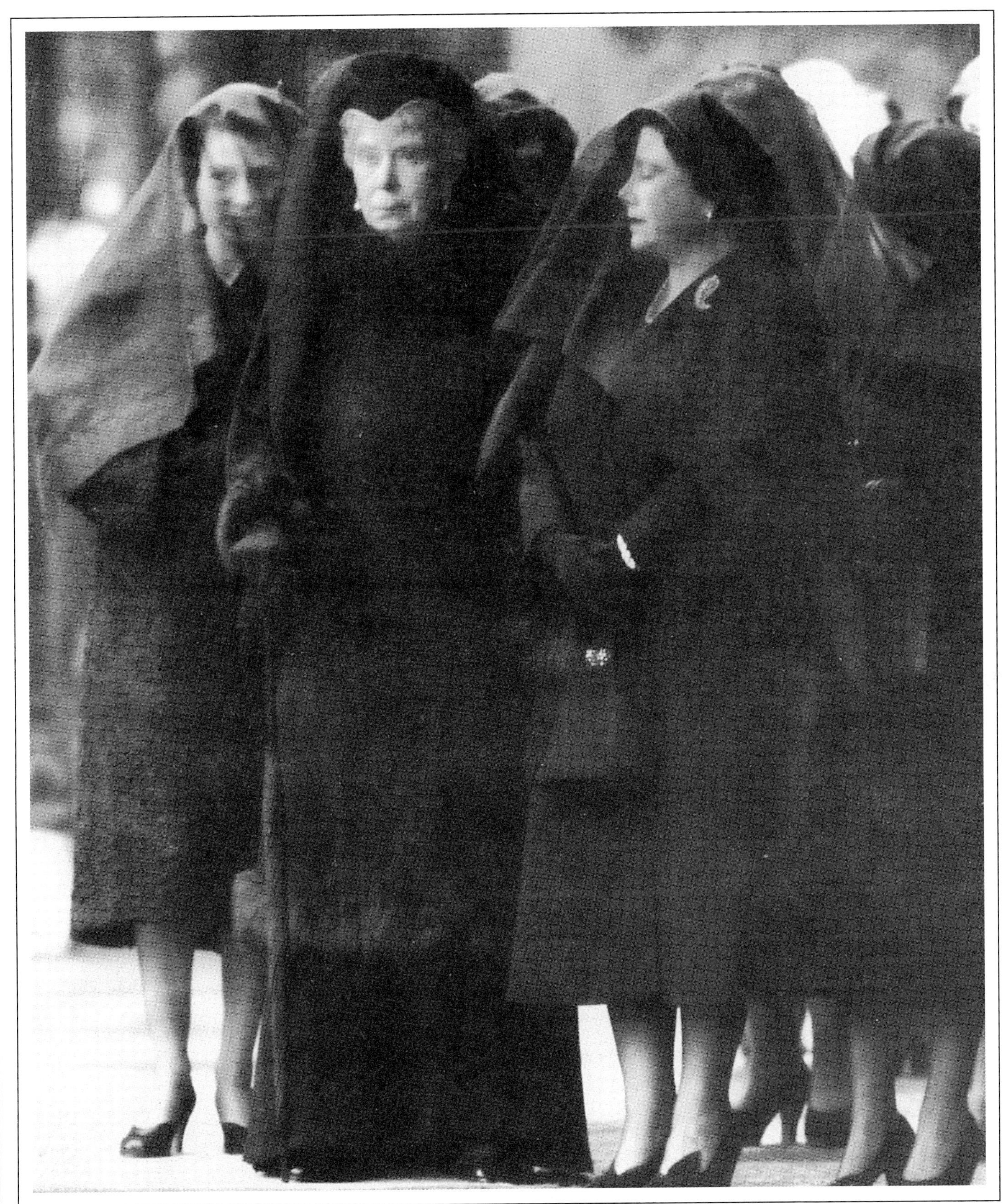

Three tragic Queens – the young Elizabeth II, Queen Mary and the Queen Mother – at the funeral of King George VI.

OPPOSITE BELOW: *Simple flowers from the gardens he loved surrounded the imposing catafalque as King George VI lay in State. Yeomen of the Guard and officers of the Household Cavalry regiments stood guard as many thousands of his subjects filed past to pay their last respects to a much-loved King.*

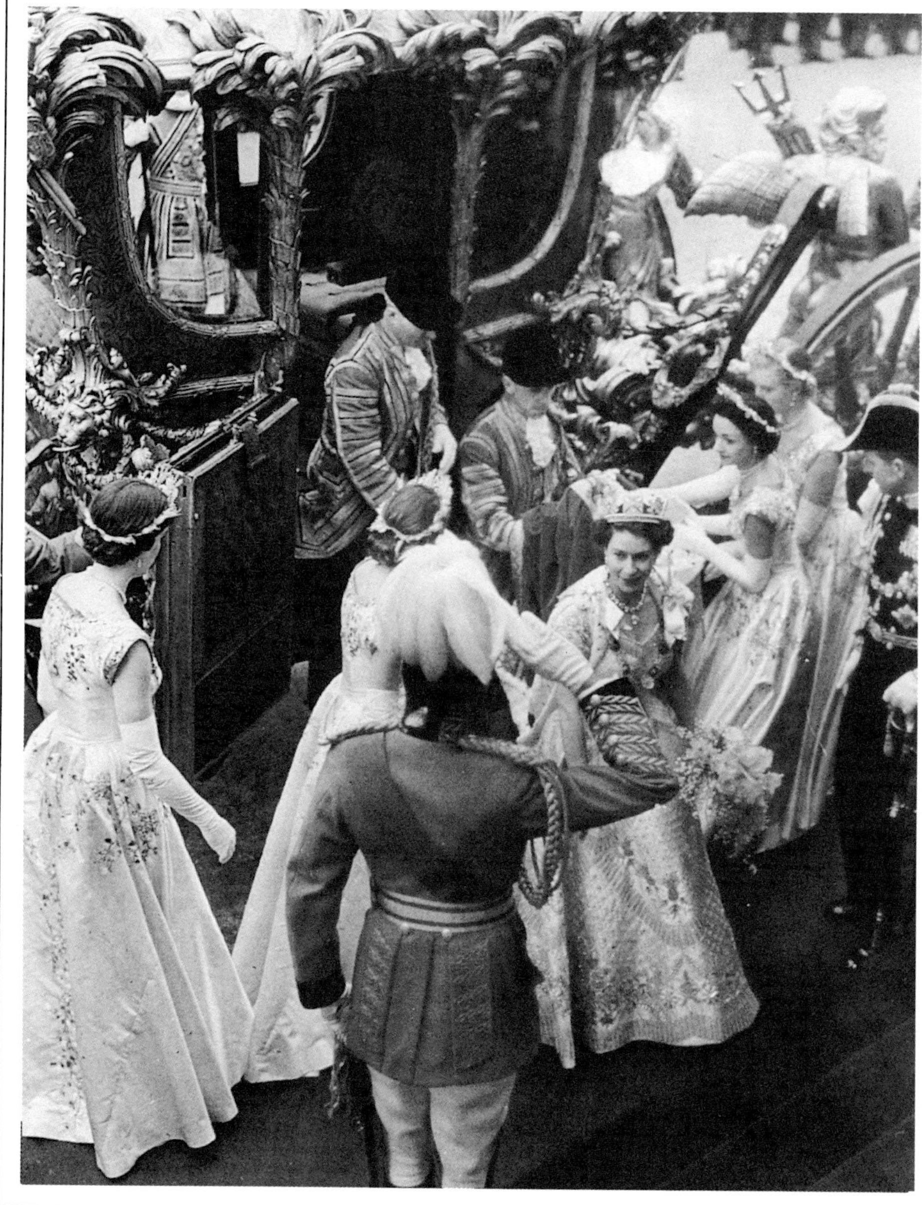

The coronation of Elizabeth II. The Queen Mother attended the ceremony wearing the same crown she had worn at her own coronation.

After dinner, Princess Margaret played the piano for her parents and then helped her father with a jigsaw puzzle. He was still laughing at one of her jokes as he said goodnight and went to bed. A night-watchman saw him fastening the latch of his window around midnight. But by next morning when his valet arrived with a cup of tea, the King was dead. He had suffered a coronary thrombosis in the small hours of the morning. The flame that had burnt so steadily and proudly throughout the tense years of war, had finally burnt out.

'I got back rather late and as I always did, rushed straight to the King's room to say that I was back and to see how he was', wrote Queen Elizabeth in a letter to Ted Seago later. 'I found him so well, so gay . . . and then I told him that you had sent the pictures back in my car and we went straight to the hall where they had been set out . . . We had a truly gay dinner with the King like his old self, and more picture-looking after dinner . . . one cannot yet believe that it has all happened, one feels rather dazed'.

Tributes from all over the world for 'a great and good King' poured into Buckingham Palace. 'Never for a moment', said Winston Churchill on the day of the King's death, 'did he fail in his duty'. The wreath sent by Prime Minister and Government was in the shape of the George Cross with a two words' tribute: 'For Gallantry'.

The night before his funeral the King lay in State in Westminster Hall and there, a few minutes before midnight, Elizabeth – now the Queen Mother – came to say a private farewell. She stood alone for almost two hours; all in black except for her pearls and a diamond brooch he had given her glinting in the subdued light, on her lapel. 'Few people realized how much she had relied on him – on his capacity for wise and detached judgement, for sound advice and how lost she now felt without him', wrote Lady Cynthia Colville, Queen Mary's lady-in-waiting.

That became all too evident as the months went by. Although she said in a statement 'My only wish is to continue the work we sought to do together', Queen Elizabeth did not, at first, find the resolve to take up her old life. She was lonely in spirit and totally desolate; so unlike her old self that those around her grew deeply concerned. She spent long, empty weeks in Scotland – back to her roots but without, at that time, any sense of purpose with which Lady Strathmore had taught her to fill her days.

In the autumn at Birkhall, a great friend, Edith Sitwell, the poet, sent her a book of her own recent work. Queen Elizabeth read the poems sitting by the river alone 'and it was a day when one felt engulfed by great black clouds of unhappiness and misery . . . thought how small and selfish is sorrow. But it bangs about until one is senseless' . . . she wrote in a letter of thanks to her friend.

It was the magic of another old friend and wartime comrade, Winston Churchill, that finally penetrated Queen Elizabeth's melancholy. She had been refusing to see visitors staying at Balmoral saying 'they won't want to see me' . . . But he took no notice and went over to Birkhall one afternoon to see 'that valiant woman'. What they said to one another, no one knows. But from that day Queen Elizabeth's smile was seen again in public and she gradually began to carve out a unique place for herself as Queen Mother.

More sad news came on 24 March 1953 when Queen Mary, another much-loved matriarch, died in her sleep.

Queen Elizabeth went to her bedside in the afternoon to say goodbye to a mother-in-law who had been her invaluable support through the years and whose passing left an irreplaceable gap in the family circle. The canny old Queen had feared death might be close and made sure that her wishes would be respected and there would be no postponement of Queen Elizabeth II's coronation on 2 June because of Court mourning.

On the day of her daughter's crowning, two men who had done so much to give her confidence in the early days as Queen – Norman Hartnell, with his fabulous clothes, and Cecil Beaton with his magical photographs – watched Queen Elizabeth's procession enter Westminster Abbey. Beaton later described 'the enormous presence and radiance of the petite Queen Mother' and Hartnell told how 'a wave of emotion passes over us' as she arrives. 'We sense what poignant memories must now be hers, recalling a like occasion when she came to be crowned Queen to the Kingship of a beloved husband'.

Perhaps it was as well she had to cope with a barage of questions from five-year-old Prince Charles in a white silk suit sitting beside her, which went on for almost an hour. It took her mind off the more emotive memories of that other coronation in 1937.

On the Palace balcony that evening Elizabeth II and her husband, the Duke of Edinburgh, stood together.

The Royal Family on the balcony of Buckingham Palace after the coronation. They are watching an RAF flypast and the Queen Mother bends to point out the planes to Charles and Anne.

The Queen and the Queen Mother in the unsaddling enclosure at Royal Ascot. The year is 1953 and the Queen has just had her first victory.

Then he turned and escorted his mother-in-law out to stand between them as the crowds roared their approval. She seemed completely back to form and it delighted everybody. But to a close friend the Queen Mother confided sadly: 'Not when I'm alone'.

But the Queen Mother has always played her part with the brilliance of a consumate actress, the talent which first showed itself at Glamis in the childhood dressing-up days. 'Of course there is something of the great actress about her', wrote Cecil Beaton, 'and in public she has to put on a show which never fails. But it is her heart and imagination which guide her'. So at the photographic session in Buckingham Palace after the coronation she was 'in rollicking spirits', whatever her innermost

In the first desolate months of her widowhood, when she was at a very low ebb, the Queen Mother found a dilapidated castle in Caithness and decided to restore it. It took nearly three years to complete the work. The Castle of Mey became the first home the Queen Mother actually owned.

thoughts. Beaton observed that 'the Queen Mother by being so basically human and understanding gives out to us a feeling of reassurance. The great mother figure and nannie to us all, through the warmth of her sympathy bathes us and wraps us in a counterpane by the fireside'. The perceptive photographer had spotted the Queen Mother's new role: that of universal grandmother.

But it was as a mother that she was most needed in the immediate future. The drama of Princess Margaret's unfulfilled love for the divorced Group Captain Peter Townsend, the late King's equerry, now comptroller of the Queen Mother's household, needed all her loving understanding and wise counsel. When the couple broke the news to her of their wish to marry, the Queen Mother – as Townsend wrote in his memoirs – 'listened with characteristic understanding – without a sign she felt angered or outraged or that she acquiesced and the Queen Mother was never anything but considerate in her attitude to me. She never once hurt either of us throughout the whole difficult affair'.

The only criticism ever heard about the Queen Mother – and it comes from her own family – is that sometimes she is 'a bit of an ostrich'. If ignoring something unpleasant will make it go away, the Queen Mother will do so. The turmoil and anguish of Margaret and Townsend was something she could very well have done without. Life was trying enough, as she tried to remake her world, as a widow. Nevertheless, the Queen Mother had been tutored in royal duty by Queen Mary and, at that time, had very strong feelings about divorce as shown by her inflexible attitude to the Duke and Duchess of Windsor. Princess Margaret's eventual decision not to marry the Group Captain, must have come as an overwhelming relief to her mother. By the end of the decade, Margaret found happiness with photographer Antony Armstrong-Jones – now Lord Snowdon. It was a marriage which gave the Queen Mother two beloved grandchildren but ended, ironically, in divorce.

For Britain's new 'Elizabethans' there was much to celebrate in coronation year and it all helped to bring the sparkle back to the Queen Mother. Everest was conquered by Sir Edmund Hillary and Sherpa Tensing on coronation day itself; Sir Gordon Richards won his first Derby; England won back the Ashes after twenty years and the nation's cheapest new car, the Ford Popular, was affordable to 'everyman' at £390 including tax.

In the first months of her widowhood the Queen Mother travelled to the furthest tip of Britain to stay with her old friends Commander and Lady Doris Vyner in Caithness. There she saw dilapidated old Castle Barrogill, and found herself going back to it again and again. 'It fascinated me', she said. Finally the Queen Mother

The first member of the Royal Family to fly in a helicopter – the Queen Mother said they transformed her life.

bought it, in order that 'its long history, its serene beauty and its proud setting' should be preserved, as she explained later. Now called the Castle of Mey, its original name, it is a small jewel of a castle – the only one of the Queen Mother's homes that she actually owns. For her it is a marvellous retreat from her busy life. 'It is tiny and enchanting with a wonderful atmosphere of peace', said one of her family. Friends believe that, among other factors in her new beginning, it was the thought of her own tough little castle, standing four square before the battering of winds from the Pentland Firth, that helped to bring stability to the second half of the Queen Mother's life.

Royal duties beckoned again as she became senior Counsellor of State during the Queen's delayed visit to Australia and New Zealand. Then in 1954 she visited America – her first major solo overseas trip. It was to receive a cheque for monies collected to commemorate King George VI. And it was there she was first dubbed 'Queen Mum' by Americans who found her irresistible and quite unlike the middle-aged widow they had expected. At Columbia University, where she received an Honorary Doctor of Law degree, they paid tribute to her courage during the war: 'A noble Queen whose quiet and constant courage in time of great stress sustained a nation and inspired a world'.

She danced the night away at the Commonwealth Ball, asking the band to play two of her current favourites: *Hey There . . . You With the Stars In Your Eyes*, and *Hernando's Hideaway*.

She went to Jamaica, going considerably out of her way to call on Noel Coward who, knowing she liked it, asked his cook to make her a curry served in coconut shells. It was apparent the famous charm was much in evidence. 'She has infinite grace of mind, charm, humour and deep-down kindness', wrote Coward, 'in addition to which she

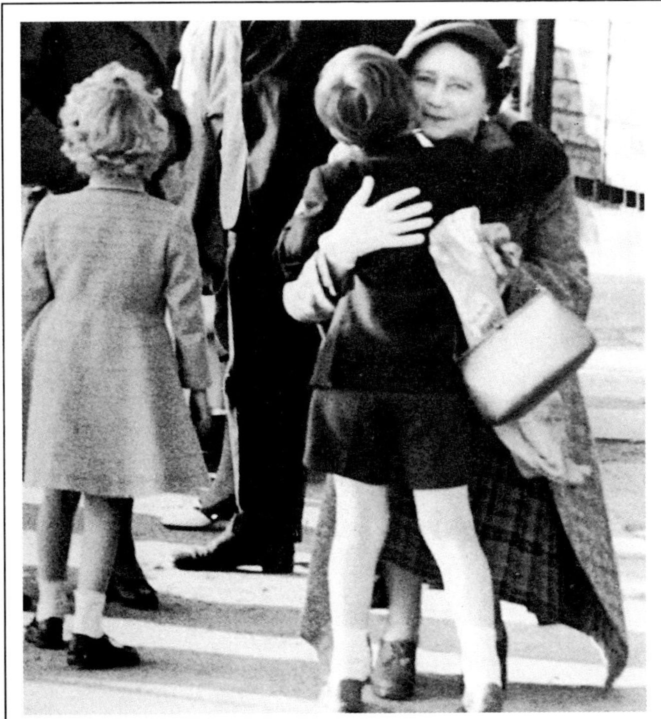

The Queen Mother welcomes Prince Charles to Scrabster Harbour, Caithness, in 1955 when he was nearly seven.

OPPOSITE ABOVE: *The Queen Mother loved highland dancing. Here she is at the Caledonian Ball giving a spirited performance of the 'Dashing White Sergeant'*

OPPOSITE BELOW: *Tiara trouble during a visit to America in 1954. Seated next to the Queen Mother at a banquet in New York is Lewis W Douglas, a former ambassador to Britain.*

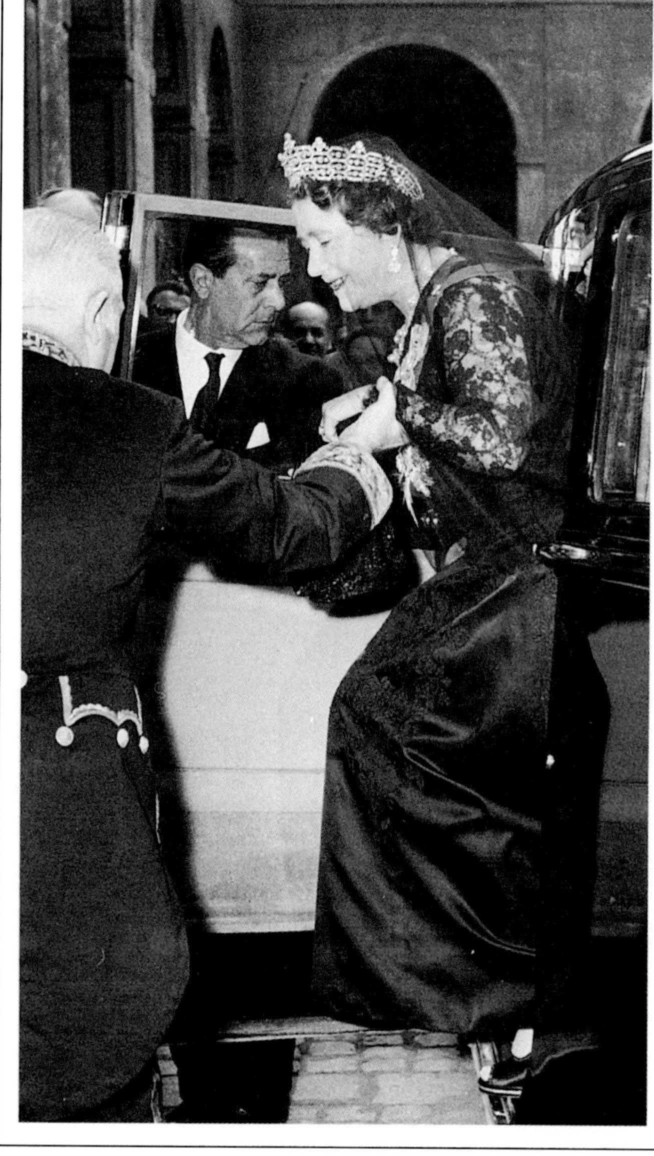

Admiring some of the glories of Rome during a visit to the Vatican Museum and St Peter's Basilica in 1959.

ABOVE RIGHT: *When the Queen Mother visited the Pope in Rome in 1959 he requested that she wear 'plenty of jewels'. She was delighted to oblige.*

looks enchanting. It was all tremendous fun and she left behind five gibbering worshippers'.

In 1955 the Queen Mother became the first woman Chancellor of London University and the first member of the Royal Family to fly in a helicopter. It became her favourite form of transport. 'The chopper has transformed my life as it did that of Anne Boleyn', she quipped.

Another first came in 1958 when she became the first of her family to circumnavigate the globe by air.

In 1959 the Queen Mother went to visit the Pope in Rome. Asking discreetly for guidance on what to wear, the Pope requested 'plenty of jewels'. Delighted, she wore masses of diamonds and her pearls, tiara and the Insignia of the Garter. 'The lot', she said, twinkling.

But rebuilding her life was easier when she was busy. It was sentimental holidays like Christmas that were difficult, despite having children and grandchildren around. To Ava, Lady Waverley, herself recently widowed, she wrote early in 1959: 'I do hope Christmas time did not make you feel too sad. It is such a thing of memories I find and one is thankful when it is over . . .'

Christmas at Sandringham at the end of the decade held a special pleasure, however. For during the holiday Princess Margaret's engagement to Antony Armstrong-Jones was sanctioned by the Queen. The Queen Mother was delighted. 'I'm so pleased you're going to marry Margaret', she told the young photographer, as she welcomed him to the family.

CHAPTER 7
DUTIES AND PLEASURES

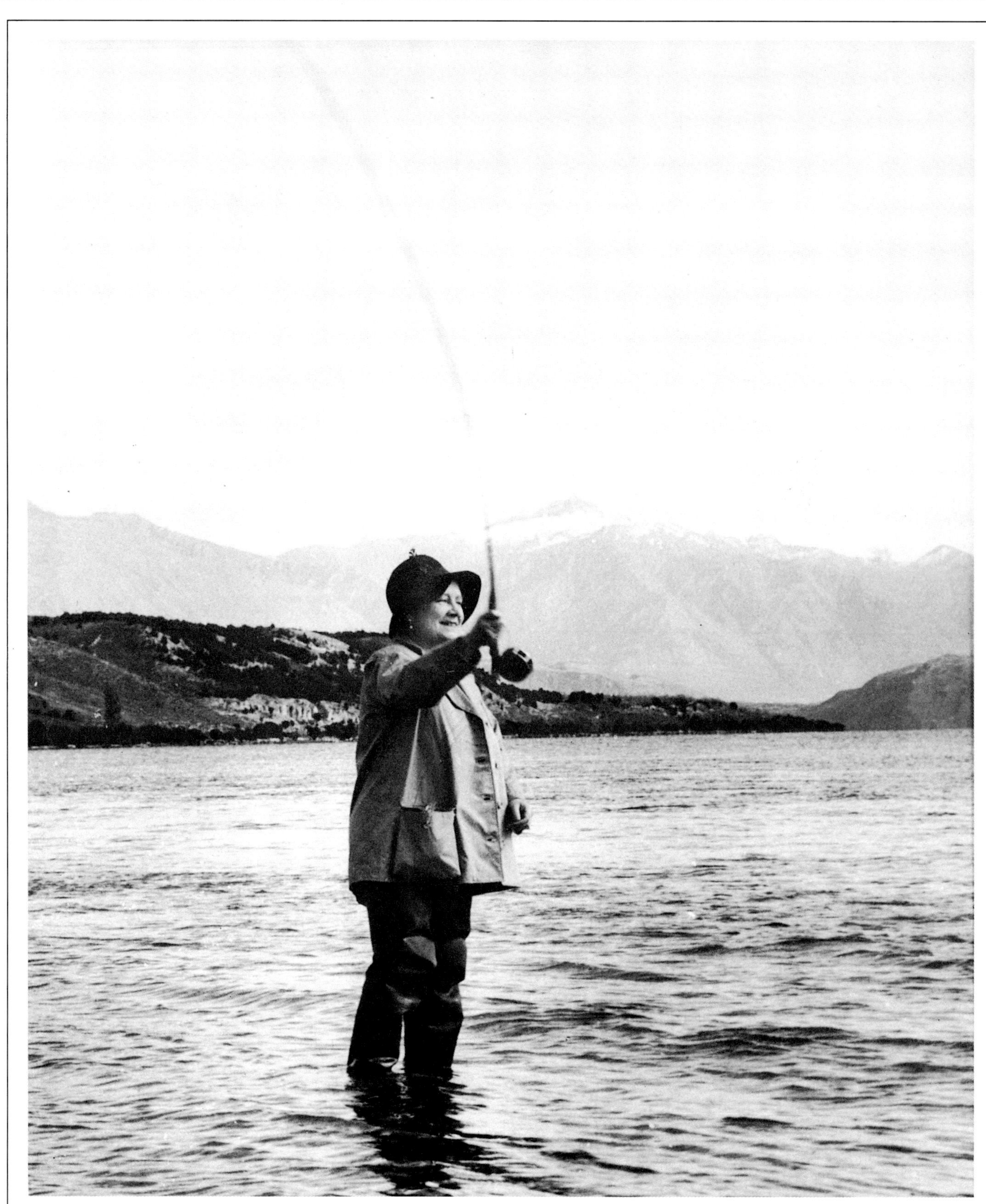

Fishing was one of the Queen Mother's greatest pleasures. Here she is casting for trout at the outlet of the Clutha River at Lake Wanaka, New Zealand in 1966.

OPPOSITE: *The New Zealanders knew of the Queen Mother's love of horses when they arranged a visit to the Inglewood Stud on South Island to see Afghanistan, an imported stallion the Queen Mother had seen racing in Britain.*

CHAPTER 7

DUTIES AND PLEASURES

THE 'Swinging Sixties' was the decade of the first heart transplant, the first man to set foot on the moon, and the first human egg to be fertilized in a test tube. A vintage harvest, indeed, from the first half of the century.

In the Queen Mother's family circle there was the unchangeable human blend of happiness and sorrow. Marriages, births and deaths punctuated the decade for the Royal Family as for any other family in the land. For the Queen Mother, herself, entering another phase of her life at sixty, it was the beginning of a period of consolidation; a reaping of the years that had gone before.

As they sang in the New Year at Sandringham, the Queen Mother knew there would be a birth in the family within a few weeks: Prince Andrew, the Queen's third child was born on 19 February; and a marriage in the late spring: Princess Margaret to Antony Armstrong-Jones on 6 May.

Life had always been an adventure but for the first time since becoming a widow, the outlook was sunny. She had reached the end of the long, dark tunnel of mourning. Nothing symbolized this state of affairs more than the centre-piece of the Queen Mother's desk at Clarence House.

Soon after the King's death her then private secretary Major Tom Harvey had the imaginative idea of asking Laurence Whistler to design something rather special as a gift for the Queen Mother. It was a crystal triptych which depicted on one side 'Duties': a microphone, scroll and foundation stone. On the other side are 'Pleasures': a pack of cards, a bottle of champagne, a fishing rod and a book of poetry. Members of the Queen Mother's household have often said: 'Ma'am, you never work or travel to please yourself' – and it was only too true. 'Work is the rent you pay for life', she tended to reply, mitigating the platitude with the twinkle in her eyes. Duty would always come first. But, in her sixties, she began to really enjoy herself in her spare time.

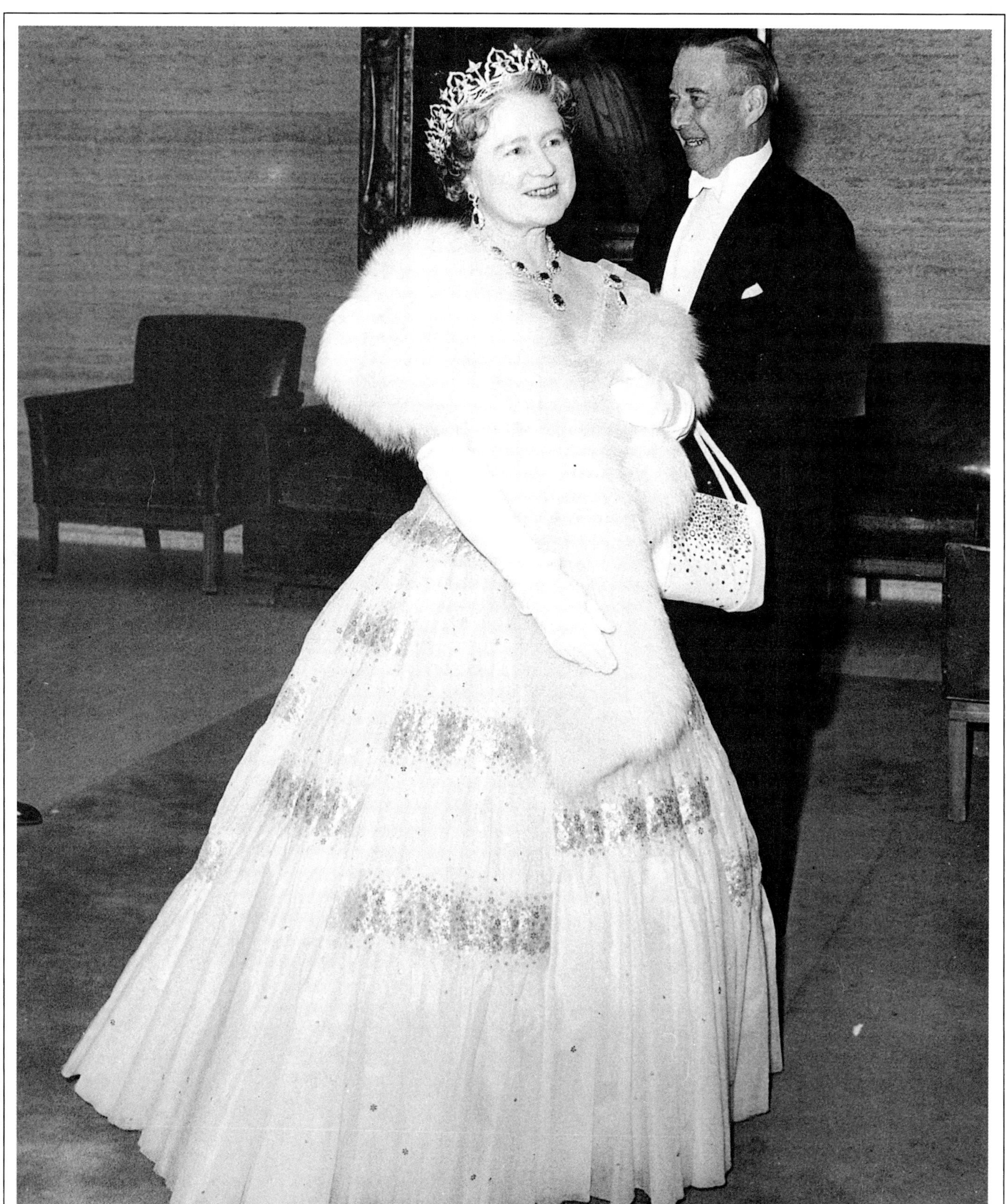

Another lovely crinoline gown. This creation was worn at the President of the Union's Dinner and Ball in 1964 after the Queen Mother became Chancellor of London University.

OPPOSITE: *Princess Margaret receives a loving smile from her mother as she and her new husband, Antony Armstrong-Jones (now Lord Snowdon), walk hand-in-hand after their wedding in Westminster Abbey in 1960.*

Racing was a great pleasure – one she shared with the Queen – and she became a regular at racecourses near London, especially if she had a horse running. Once or twice a year her small figure, usually muffled in mackintosh, headscarf over a hat and wellington boots, could be seen, often buffeted by an icy wind and driving rain, as she watched the gallops at her trainer's, the late Peter Cazalet's Fairlawne stables near Lingfield racecourse.

The Sixties were very successful steeplechasing years for the Queen Mother and racegoers grew used to seeing her mingling with – and often being accidentally jostled – by the crowds at a racecourse as she made her way to the paddock. As one sporting writer put it: 'If there is a shorter cut to a bloody nose in Tattersalls than to criticize the Queen Mother in any way, I do not know it'.

The crowds were probably even more bitterly disappointed than the Queen Mother when her horse Devon Loch, well in the lead in the 1956 Grand National, collapsed just thirty yards from the winning post. Dick Francis, the jockey, now a best-selling thriller writer, was in tears after the incident but the Queen Mother just said philosophically: 'That's racing'. Then she went over to her horse, stroked him and said: 'Dear, poor boy'. Later she gave Francis a silver cigarette box engraved 'Devon Loch's National' with a private message inside the lid he would not let anyone see.

The Queen Mother really loved her horses and was especially touched when during a stay in hospital in 1964 after an appendix operation, flowers arrived from two of her horses, Rip and Double Star. The 'loving and grateful owner' thanked them in a letter, 'for this imaginative, amusing and beautiful present'.

Apart from her many official overseas trips, the Queen Mother loved going to France on private visits. She enjoyed the food and wine, spoke the language beautifully – thanks to childhood governesses – and enjoyed the ambience. At least once a year she took a small party across the Channel. On one occasion she rented an old house in Provence; on another she took over one floor of a hotel and she often stayed with friends such as the Rothschilds at Château Mouton in the Médoc. During one trip to Burgundy, someone gave her a tiny mouth organ and in the evening a local choir came to the château in which she was staying. The Queen Mother listened to their singing from her bedroom window. Suddenly she remembered her present and, as the choir sang, she played their Burgundian tunes back to them on the mouth organ.

Princess Margaret's wedding was a day of great happiness. Though the marriage has since ended in divorce, the Queen Mother remained fond of Lord Snowdon and adored her two grandchildren, Viscount Linley and Lady Sarah Chatto.

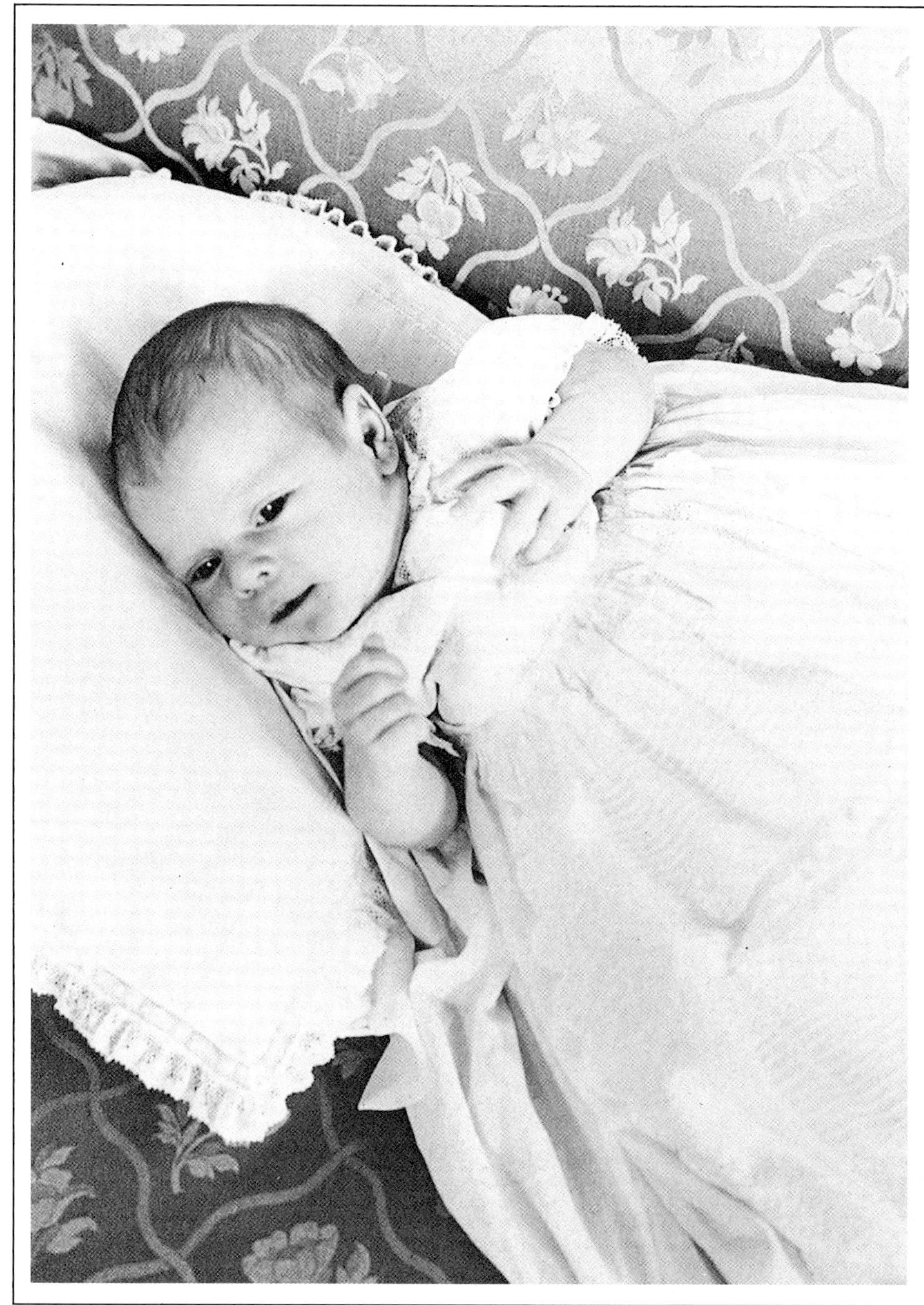

The infant Prince Andrew by Cecil Beaton.

Sometime after the wedding, Margaret and Tony took the Queen Mother to spend the evening in the small Rotherhithe room, rented from journalist Robert Glenton, where they had done much of their courting. Princess Margaret and her mother sang and played the piano while Tony cooked dinner. The Queen Mother threw crumbs of her bread roll to the swans on the Thames. The party broke up after midnight with a spirited rendering of La Marseillaise as a French ship passed by. 'I've not enjoyed an evening so much since I was twenty', the Queen Mother was heard to remark afterwards.

The following year brought sorrow with the death of her elder sister Mary, followed in the autumn by that of David, her inseparable childhood companion, while he was staying at Birkhall with his sister.

The Sixties saw two more Windsor family weddings: the Duke of Kent to Katharine Worsley in 1961 and Princess Alexandra to the Hon (now Sir) Angus Ogilvy in 1963. He was the grandson of Lady Airlie, Queen Mary's lady-in-waiting who had done so much to foster the romance of Elizabeth and Bertie.

The 'Year of the Babies' came in 1964 when the Queen had another son, Prince Edward; Princess Margaret had a

BUCKINGHAM PALACE

11 March 1964

The Queen has had a comfortable night.

Her Majesty and the baby are both well.

RIGHT: Following the birth of Prince Edward in 1964, Buckingham Palace kept the world informed of his progress.

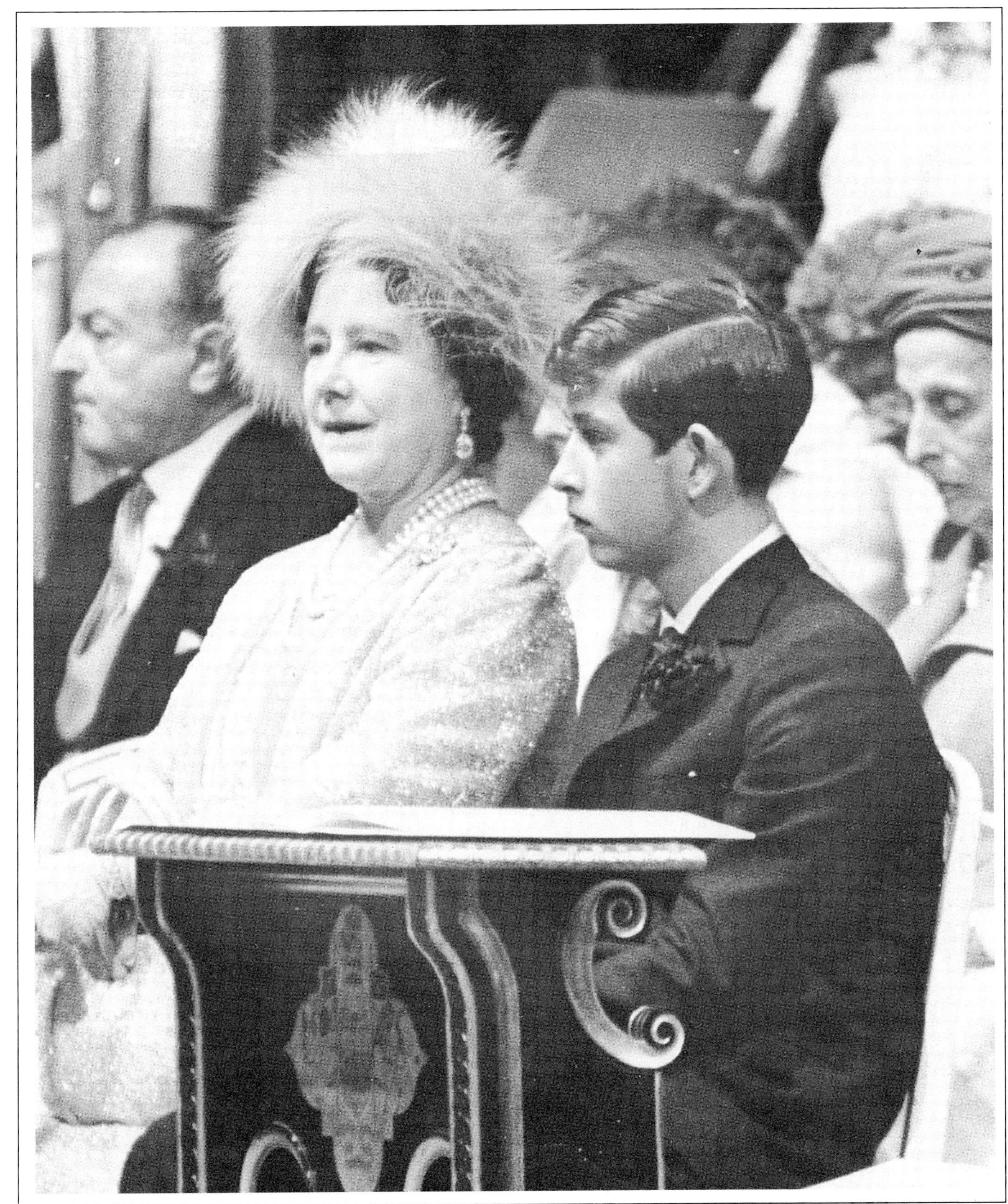

The Queen Mother and Prince Charles at the wedding of Princess Alexandra of Kent and the Honourable (now Sir) Angus Ogilvy in Westminster Abbey – one of the many family weddings during the Sixties.

The Queen Mother receives her declaration of election to the office of Chancellor of the University of London in 1965.

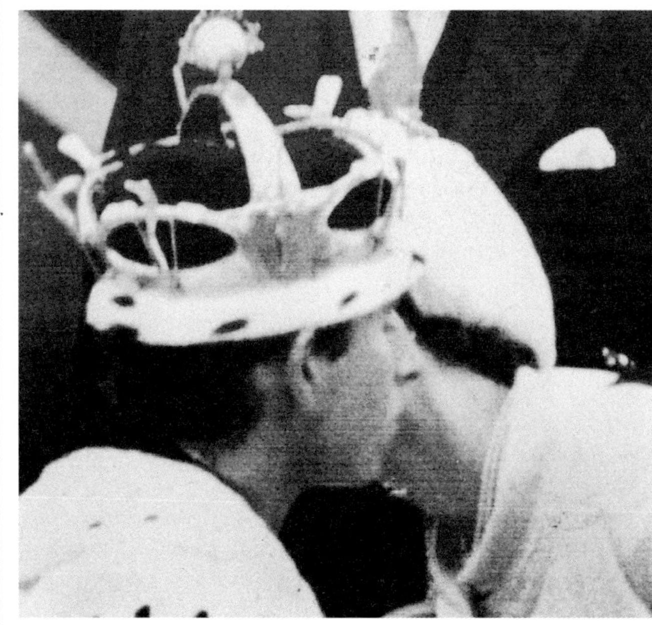

A kiss from the Queen for the new Prince of Wales – July 1969.

daughter, Sarah; Princess Alexandra gave birth to a son, James; and the Duchess of Kent, a daughter, Helen.

In December 1966, the Queen Mother attended an evening reception at St James's Palace and then went straight into the King Edward VII Hospital for Officers for major abdominal surgery. By coincidence the operation was carried out on 10 December, the anniversary of the abdication. The bulletin said she was 'comfortable' but the Queen Mother said wryly: 'There is all the difference in the patient's meaning of the word and the surgeon's'.

By June of that same year, on the anniversary of the D-Day landings, she was back on duty, retracing the late King's steps and visiting the beaches as her husband did soon after the invasion.

Fishing was another of the Queen Mother's great 'Pleasures'. She and David had fished with bent pins and worms on the lake at The Bury, and since then she has fished the royal waters at Balmoral for salmon. Until very recently she was still wading waist high into the river Dee and a favourite family story is of one night when she did not return for dinner. Her household and guests grew alarmed and a search party was organized complete with hurricane lamps. They found the Queen Mother on her way home carrying a twenty-pound salmon and looking extremely pleased with herself. 'This is what took me so long', she said.

The toll of family deaths began again in 1967 when two sisters-in-law, the Princess Royal, the Queen Mother's old 'guiding' friend of pre-marriage days, and Princess Marina of Kent both died suddenly. No sooner were those funerals over than there was another: the Queen Mother's beloved elder sister Rose, Countess Granville, who had run the Glamis hospital – the last of her brothers and sisters. Queen Elizabeth observed sorrowfully that she was now the only one left of her generation of the Bowes Lyon family.

A visit to Smithfield meat market in 1968 revived memories when the porters spontaneously began singing to her: 'If you were the only girl in the world . . .' 'I must listen to this', she said and stayed for a singsong. 'I think she was very touched by it', said one of the men. 'She had tears in her eyes at the end. Suddenly we realized we were singing to the Queen Mother'. For her part, had her mind swung back to the evenings at Glamis, during the First World War, when she was a young girl and sang that same song with the men back from the trenches?

The Sixties ended with a flourish and a spectacular pageant with her grandson as its star. At the Investiture of the Prince of Wales, the Queen Mother watched with special pride as he paid homage to his mother and sovereign against the dramatic backdrop of Edward I's Caernarvon Castle.

CHAPTER 8
GREAT-GRANDMOTHER

The Queen Mother became the 160th (and first woman in 900 years) Warden of the Cinque Ports at Dover Castle in 1979. To witness the ceremony and to join the party on Britannia *afterwards she took along her grandchildren Prince Edward, Viscount Linley and Lady Sarah Armstrong-Jones.*

CHAPTER 8
GREAT-GRANDMOTHER

GOLD candelabra in the ballroom were filled with tobacco plants and zinnias and a whole flowering syringa tree – a shrub much-loved by the Queen Mother – was planted in an enormous malachite pot in the Supper Room, for a very special party at Windsor Castle. It was the prelude to the Queen Mother's eighth decade – a glamorous ball given by the Queen in May as a celebration of her mother's seventieth birthday, three months later. Also fêted on that occasion in the floodlit castle were the Duke of Gloucester – whom, sadly, illness prevented from attending – Earl Mountbatten and the Duke of Beaufort who all shared the honours of the evening because, they too, were as old as the century.

In pale, misty chiffon shimmering with sequins complemented by her favourite diamond and pearl necklace and tiara, the Queen Mother waltzed with her eldest grandson, Prince Charles. He has taken the place of the son she never had and, from the moment as a toddler when he first looked for butterscotch in her handbag, they have been devoted to each other.

The Queen Mother anguished as he struggled through spartan Gordonstoun, telling friends when he had finished his education: 'Now he doesn't need to be toughened any more'. But, typically, when Charles appealed to her to intercede on his behalf because he hated it so, she replied: 'I cannot do anything about it but I'll help you get through it'. So she found reasons for going to Scotland more often and visited her grandson with parcels of 'goodies' and other treats. He reminds her of her husband and his grandfather, King George VI. There is the same quiet thoughtfulness, kindness and diffidence; the same disinclination to inherit a kingdom. But immensely comforting though she was, the Queen Mother's inherent unpunctuality often meant he was in trouble for returning to school late. On one occasion his grandmother telephoned to apologize: 'I'm so sorry to have got him back late – but you know what grannies can be like!'

The Seventies saw the birth of the revolutionary aeroplane 'Concorde' and the first test-tube baby. It was also the decade when the Queen celebrated her Silver Jubilee, the Duke of Windsor died, Princess Margaret was divorced and Princess Anne married Captain Mark Phillips and they gave the Queen Mother her first great-grandchild when Peter Phillips was born on 15 November 1977. At the Buckingham Palace christening were five generations of the Royal Family: the Queen Mother's daughters, grandchildren, the new great-grandchild and Princess Alice, Countess of Athlone, last surviving grandchild of Queen Victoria.

The Queen Mother found, in her seventies, that she was growing increasingly interested in the young. Her own family circle included Prince Charles and Princess Anne, then in their twenties, and four younger grandchildren: Prince Andrew, Prince Edward and Princess Margaret's two, David Viscount Linley and Lady Sarah Armstrong-Jones. For someone who loves looking forward, the younger generation presented a more optimistic future than her own contemporaries. 'You look in the marriages and birth columns for your friends', she observed to Princess Anne some years later. 'For me, it is the other one. They are all going upstairs'. Among them was her brother-in-law, the Duke of Windsor. His funeral on 5 June 1972, meant another meeting with the Duchess which was something the Queen Mother would have avoided had it been possible.

The years had not dimmed her feelings about the Windsors. 'If there is a chink in her armour it is if anyone mentions the abdication', said one of her family. In the event, the tragic figure of the heavily sedated Duchess brought a sympathetic responsiveness from members of the Royal Family, particularly from Prince Charles. The Queen Mother took her arm and said: 'I know how you feel. I've been through it myself'. The Duchess's doctor who had stayed close to her throughout the ordeal of the funeral was in a position to observe the meeting between the two women, now the only two living members of the cast that played out the drama of the abdication. 'Her Majesty was kindness itself', he said afterwards.

Three royal ladies with a shared interest: Princess Anne, the Queen Mother and the Queen watch an incident at the start of the 1971 Derby.

At the Badminton Horse Trials a lady in the crowd lent the Queen Mother her coat so that she could sit on the damp grass.

It is not only her own grandchildren who adored the Queen Mother. To the Duke and Duchess of Kent's eldest son, the Earl of St Andrews, she was always 'a shining light', just as she was to his cousin Charles. When George and his wife Sylvana, a Roman Catholic divorcee, were married in a Register Office, no one was kinder than the Queen Mother who attended their service of blessing at St James's Chapel, when the Queen – as head of the church – felt that she could not. Prince William, elder son of the Duke and Duchess of Gloucester, who was so tragically killed in an air crash in 1972, was also extremely close to 'Aunt Elizabeth'. He once said to journalist Audrey Whiting: 'If I let myself down – say I get into a mess of some sort – my first thought would be that the Queen Mother would feel that I let her down. I have always felt like this even as a young child. It isn't that she ever said anything. It's a sort of indescribable sense of dedication she gave me'.

It is that sense of dedication that the Queen Mother helped to instil in the Prince of Wales and, increasingly, in his former wife. Diana showed more and more, gentle compassion and the courage to face up to the tragedies she met in her public duties which balanced the beautiful fashion-plate image of earlier years. She became aware, as she grew more mature, of facts of life more often brushed under the welcoming carpet on royal visits. In her increased commitment to her duty the late Princess of Wales, was obviously influenced not only by her mother-in-law the Queen but by those two marvellous great-grandmothers, the Queen Mother and her own grandmother the late Ruth Lady Fermoy. She was a woman-of-the-bedchamber to the Queen Mother and an old and trusted friend. As a role model for the Queen Consort she was expected to be, Diana needed to look no further than the Queen Mother who had already helped her emergence as Princess of Wales and from whose house she was married. The Queen Mother exuded a sense of timelessness Diana was expected to acquire after decades of looking over her shoulder at history and helping to make it herself. 'Darling, you just grow into the job', the Queen Mother assured a still-nervous Princess after her first few months as a royal.

However great the problems to be faced the royal matriarch was a sheet-anchor for all her grandchildren and the circle of Windsor and Bowes Lyon nephews and nieces with whom she regularly kept in touch. 'She is a very family person; tremendously realistic and on the ball about us all', her great-niece Lady Elizabeth Anson told me. 'Fascinated by the job one does and full of admiration for a working person'. 'Amazing what you've done', the Queen Mother would say to young royals like her grandson David Linley, who started a furniture-making business, now of international repute, and to his sister Sarah who is a professional artist and studied at the National Gallery School.

As grandmothers do, the world over, the Queen Mother often entertained her younger relatives with stories about her childhood. They have heard all about the Enchanted Wood of her Hertfordshire home and the capers she and her brother David got up to at Glamis. When

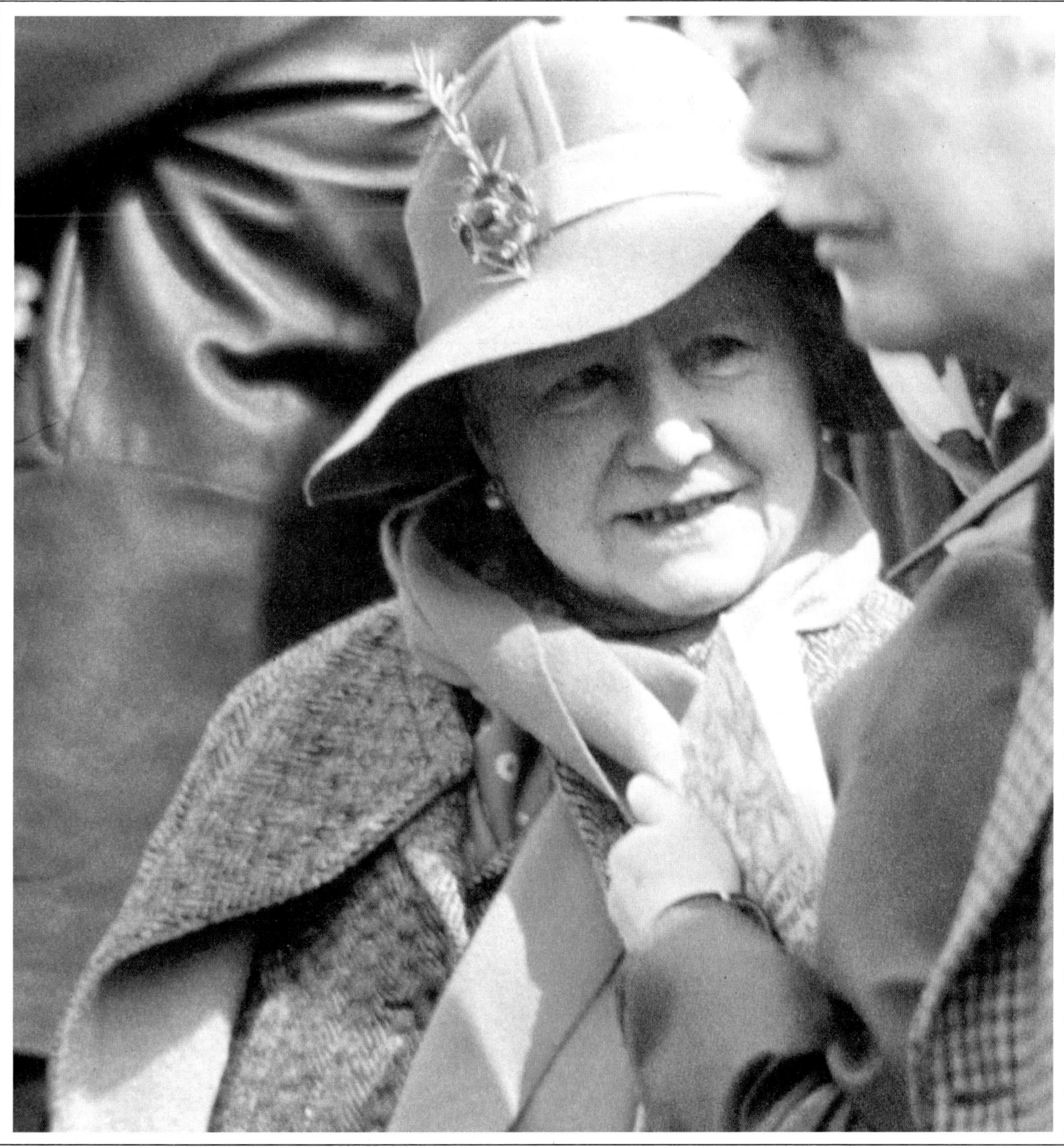

The Queen Mother in her favourite misty blue. She pulled her hat well down in the blustery wind, and wore a warm scarf, at the races.

Prince William, heir to the throne after his father Prince Charles, told her excitedly that he was flying up to Scotland, she talked about the wonderful trips of her girlhood by train, 'Do you know', she said once, 'I once made a banana last the whole journey'. Brother David had bet her she would not have the will power.

'All the family know that if something's a bit dull, her eyes twinkle and she says: "Now, what shall we do next?" Suddenly everything seems like fun again', said her great-niece, some years before her death.

Off-duty at the Badminton Horse Trials: the Queen Mother with the Queen and Princess Margaret.

Each September the Queen Mother threw a party for the younger royals and their friends at Birkhall. A band was hired from Aberdeen and they danced the light northern night away with the still-graceful royal great-grandmother as the star performer. 'She loves to learn all the new dances but, to please her, there are masses of reels as well' said one of the family at the time.

In August 1979 the Queen Mother was installed as Lord Warden of the Cinque Ports and Constable of Dover Castle, following such great names as Wellington and Churchill. On that historic occasion she took three of her grandchildren – Prince Edward, the Queen's youngest, and David and Sarah, Princess Margaret's children – with her on the royal yacht *Britannia*.

Later that month came tragedy of the sort that permanently haunts the Royal Family. Earl Mountbatten, their 'grandfather' figure was assassinated on 27 August while on holiday in Ireland. It was a devastating shock for the Prince of Wales who had adored his 'honorary grandfather'. His father, the Duke of Edinburgh, deeply upset himself but made of tougher emotional fibre, masked his feelings with the traditional British 'stiff upper lip'. Perhaps to hide his own grief he reacted testily to his eldest son's despair. But to the Queen Mother he was her husband Bertie all over again and she comforted Charles as she had King George VI in the bad times. Although she had been widowed for twenty-seven years, the Queen Mother still grieved for the King and was able to understand her grandson's desolation and bitterness, whereas his father could not. The Queen Mother did not regard tears and emotion in men as a weakness, as her son-in-law does, but knew – as her husband had proved so conclusively – that they are no handicap to courage.

There had always been a close bond between the Queen Mother and the Prince of Wales, but, as the Eighties approached it became an even more devoted and unique relationship. A gardener all her life she introduced Charles to two great loves – gardening and fishing. When he was quite small she taught him to cast a line from the high lawns of Birkhall and his love of plants, trees and vegetables, was first nurtured in his grandmother's four beautiful gardens. Homoeopathy, of which the Queen Mother has always been a supporter, interested Charles too and led him to campaign for greater acceptance of the benefits of alternative medicine. And, finally, at the end of the decade, with her old Aberdeenshire friend, Ruth Lady Fermoy, she helped to find him a wife.

CHAPTER 9
INDIAN SUMMER

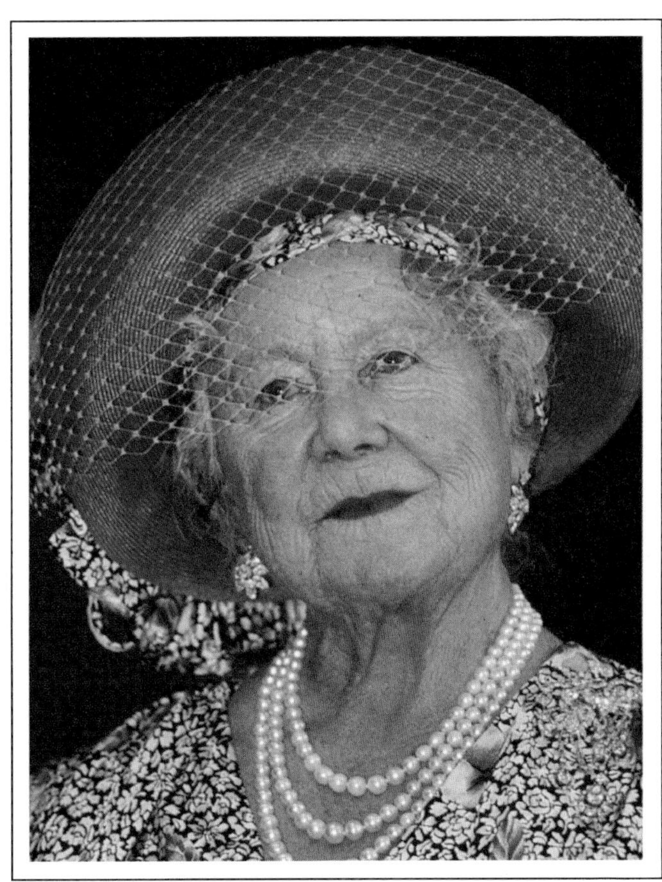

The controversial portrait of the Queen Mother by Alison Watt. Many thought it totally unlike the smiling, happy royal grandmother the public was used to seeing. But there were those who recognized the look. Behind the comfortable facade the Queen Mother presented to the world was an astute and formidable character. 'A law unto herself', as one of her family put it. But she always cloaked her strength with gentleness.

CHAPTER 9

INDIAN SUMMER

THE small figure in the mackintosh and wellington boots with a scarf tied over an old, rather battered hat, stood on the pebbly beach at Mey, where the horizon stretches away towards the outline of Orkney, singing an old Highland song. 'Will ye no come back again', she crooned, trying to raise her voice above the wind and coax the black heads of the seals inland. Queen Elizabeth, the Queen Mother, was relaxing

On the Palace balcony after her eightieth birthday Thanksgiving Service.

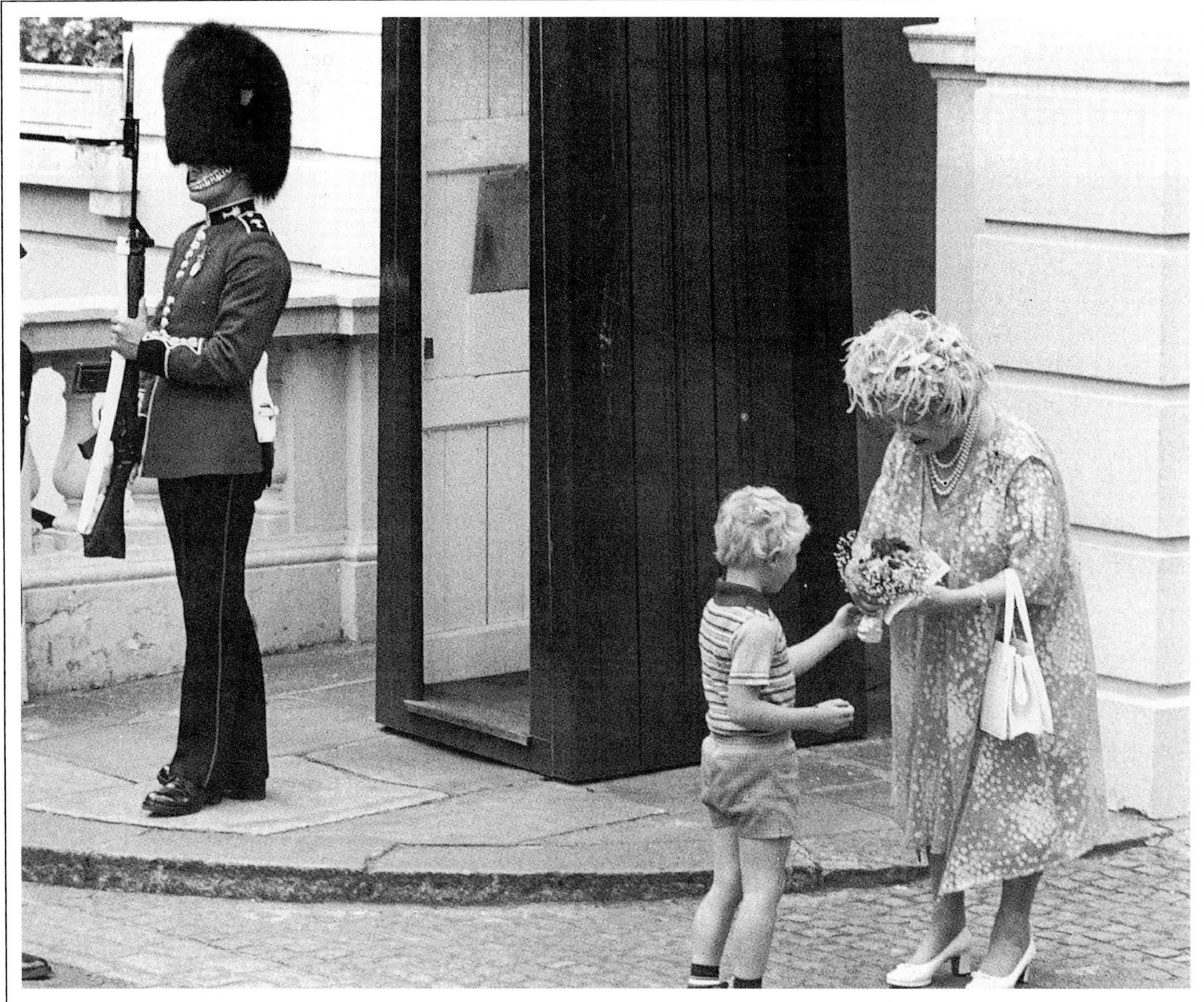

The Queen Mother accepted a posy from a young admirer outside Clarence House, her London home, on the occasion of her eightieth birthday. The Irish Guardsman giving the royal salute and the casually dressed lad capture two aspects of the Queen Mother's life – the pomp and ceremony accorded to majesty and the warmth and affection given to a much-loved 'Queen Mum'.

after the hectic and exciting summer of her eightieth birthday celebrations. Only two days before thousands had given her an ecstatic welcome as she drove with the Prince of Wales to a great Service of Thanksgiving at St Paul's Cathedral. Now, in the peace of her remote haven in Caithness where she had hastened after the celebrations, there was time to meditate on the long, fulfilling life that had brought her to her ninth decade.

But not for long. All through the Eighties the Queen Mother continued to fill her small castle with guests during her August visit. Most of them much younger than herself and so their hostess devised energetic and amusing activities to pass the time. At the end of each visit she gave a small dance for the house party and local guests which usually ended with the Queen Mother leading a long conga-line out of her oak-panelled front door on to a lawn where daisies were allowed to grow because she liked them.

The Castle of Mey is the only one of her homes that the Queen Mother actually owned and, significantly, it was in her bedroom there that she installed one of her most precious possessions: a small white fireplace with, as its only decoration, a medallion in the shape of a heart. It was a sentimental birthday present from the late King, given because he knew how much importance she placed on 'hearth and home'. It was moved first from Buckingham Palace to Clarence House when she became a widow, then to Mey when she bought the ancient castle at the far end of Britain. The carefree hospitality in Caithness was echoed in all her homes, although entertaining was more formal in London, at Clarence House. Most guests considered the Queen Mother's parties to be the best in town, whether at teatime in the Garden Room; elegant luncheons in 'the *salons vertes*', as she called the shady rooms created by the ancient plane trees in the garden; or supper parties after the theatre beneath the chandeliers in the dining-room where portraits of George III and his children hang on the warm apricot walls. Contemporaries and, sadly, there were few of them left, struggled to keep up with the Queen Mother admiring the stamina which would not give in to the limitations age too often imposes. 'My mother comes from an amazing generation', said the Queen.

She would never admit to being cold or tired, loved rain and wind ('a strong wind will blow the germs away', as her mother used to say). 'I've never seen her tired or edgy', said Lady Elizabeth Anson, when the Queen Mother was ninety. 'She is the most energetic person always and thinks nothing of tramping miles with her dogs'. But walking more slowly, then, to the relief of those accompanying the royal progress. But although she ignored the elements herself, the Queen Mother was the first to be concerned if others looked miserable. 'Heavens you must be cold, darling', she said to her great-niece who had arrived at Royal Lodge soaked, after a drenching walk back from church. 'You must have a drink to warm you up. Shall I pour it? Or do pour it yourself?'

Exploring country churches was a pastime first introduced to the Queen Mother by the late Poet Laureate Sir John Betjeman who was a dear friend. She often suggested such an expedition to weekend guests after lunch on Sunday and a small but interesting church in the Home Counties got an unexpected royal visit.

Prince Andrew's return from the Falklands brought rejoicing to the Royal Family. Like his mother, the Queen, the Queen Mother agonized during the months he fought in the conflict.

But it was her unshakeable belief in family life and its impact as a national example that was such an important part of the Queen Mother's influence through the years. 'The most marvellous mother', said the Queen, 'always standing back and never interfering'. An interesting comment which underlies how gently and tactfully the Queen Mother's undoubted authority had been dispensed without even the faintest suggestion of matriarchal bossiness. She was, of course, taught the importance of a warm, caring family circle by her mother of whom it was once said: 'If there be a genius for family life she has it'. This gift was handed down in full measure to her daughter who brought to a Royal Family starved of demonstrative, loving affection, a vibrant warmth and happiness which the painter Pietro Annigoni described years later as 'an inner beauty'. It's all very well to look glamorous on the surface, but without that personal quality your subject is nothing but a dummy', he observed. 'The Queen Mother is one of the loveliest people I have ever met. It is hard to imagine a kinder, warmer, more appealing human being – she is absolutely perfect'. The searching eyes of the painter saw that the Queen Mother had a personal quality which transcended rank or beauty. But those who were really close to her knew that beneath the smiling face and diminutive form there was strength as inflexible as the Grampian Mountains near her Glamis family home. 'She was highly determined and a law unto herself', said one of her family who knew her well. 'But she made her point in a very gentle way'. If displeased, she made no effort to hide it. 'Mummy's in a difficult mood today', the Queen was heard to comment to her sister. But to the public, the 'Queen Mum' always appeared reassuringly the same. A happy, waving, comfortable 'People's Grandmother' – the role she exchanged with that of Queen Consort when she became a widow. 'But it is what lay beneath the surface that is so interesting', said one who had known her for many years. 'She could be formidable – although few saw it'.

There were glimpses in her handling of a dissident student who tore up his graduation certificate just presented to him by the Queen Mother as the first woman Chancellor of London University. Instead of disdainfully ignoring it, as her daughter would have done, she fixed the lad with a steely gaze. 'I'd like to meet that young man', she said icily, 'and tell him I don't like litter'. On another occasion the glint in those hyacinth blue eyes, usually so gentle and twinkling, would have been a warning to anyone who knew her well. Seeing some youths throwing stones at cars driving through Windsor Great Park, she stopped her own and advanced upon them purposefully, to her detective's dismay. Her tiny figure cosily wrapped in misty-blue tweed, a feathered concoction on her grey curls, she looked at them sternly: 'I don't mind you throwing stones at me', she said tartly, 'but whatever will the American tourists think?' The truants scattered, mumbling apologies and the Queen Mother continued serenely on her way to have tea with the Queen at the castle.

Nowhere was the Queen Mother's gentle but firm influence shown more decisively than in her support for her grandson's wooing of Lady Diana Spencer, granddaughter of her old friend Ruth Fermoy. There are some who firmly believe that the two distinguished old ladies put their heads together and carefully plotted the courtship of a future king and queen. It is well known that the Queen Mother offered the hospitality of her Scottish home, Birkhall, to her grandson and Diana in December 1980, so that they could be together for a few days before they spent Christmas apart – a strong indication of how much she favoured the match. When Prince Charles proposed and was accepted a few weeks before the official engagement was announced, he and Diana immediately telephoned their two grandmothers at Clarence House to tell them the news. On the evening of their engagement on 24 February 1981, they had a celebration dinner with the Queen Mother and Lady Fermoy at Clarence House and Diana moved in the following day for a few weeks of intensive 'royal' coaching.

Her other grandchildren also kept closely in touch. 'Can I bring some friends round to meet you,' said a young voice on the telephone. 'That would be such fun', replied the Queen Mother, using one of her favourite expressions. Then she ordered an especially rich chocolate cake for five o'clock tea in the Garden Room. The Queen Mother loved these impromptu calls, the ones the operator called 'specials' that were put straight through to her pale blue sitting-room. Another was the one that came, regular as clockwork, from whichever part of the world the Queen might be at the time. The two Elizabeths spoke every morning and in many ways the Queen Mother was as close to the heart of Palace affairs as she ever was as Consort. 'Your Majesty, Her Majesty is on the line' said the operator who enjoyed this important moment almost as much as either of them.

The Queen Mother was a wonderful letter writer and if any of her correspondence is ever published will form a sparkling record of the events that were a part of her life in the twentieth century. 'At Christmas', said Lady Elizabeth Anson, 'she personally writes every envelope for her Christmas cards'. For most of us it is a chore but to her it is a labour of love.

The Queen Mother's generation were taught as children never to mention the food when a guest at luncheon or dinner – it simply was not done. But she

Four generations of the House of Windsor: the Queen Mother holding Prince William, flanked by the Queen and the Prince of Wales at the baby's christening on 4 August 1982 – the Queen Mother's birthday.

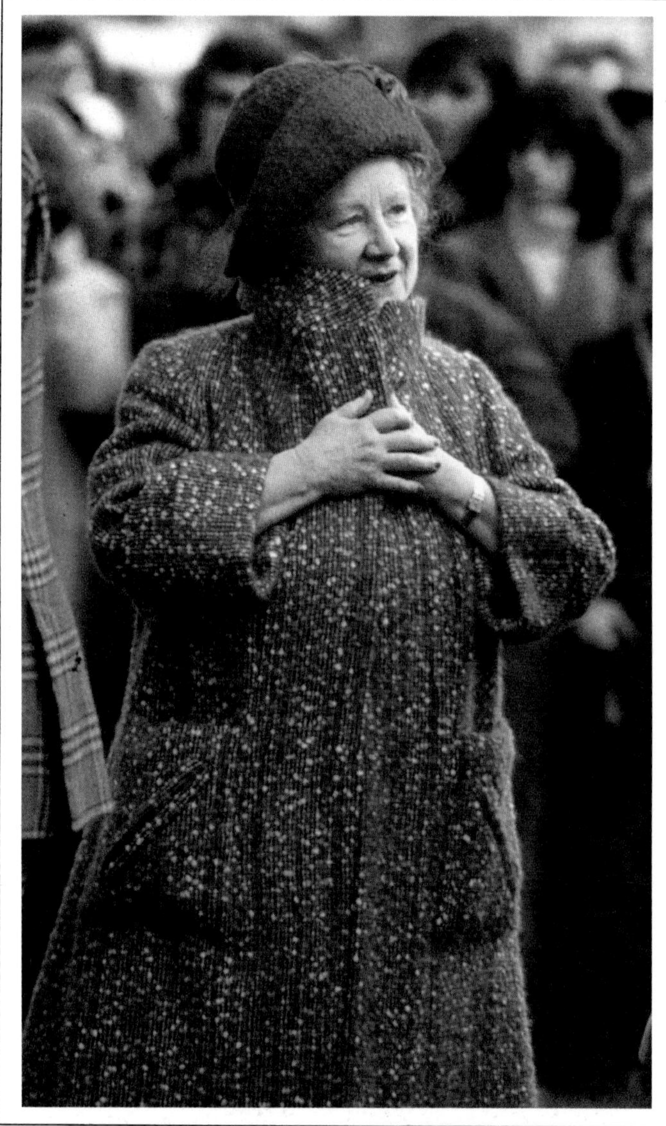

Arriving at Wolferton Church, near Sandringham.

The British Embassy in Oslo, 1983.

always did: 'How delicious', she would say using another favourite expression, 'I simply must have the recipe'. She had a habit, if the party was threatening to be boring, of being 'almost provocative – not risqué exactly but mischievous'. She would often end a typically hesitant sentence with a question, her head on one side: 'Don't you think?'

As a hostess the Queen Mother was superlative and always served exceptional food and wine. But pre-lunch drinks could be dangerous; 'frightfully strong', said one nervous guest who, because it was in a large tumbler thought her drink innocuous only to find, as she giggled her way through lunch, that it had been a mammoth martini cocktail. The Queen Mother often served the drinks herself, particularly when it was 'family' and the butler was rarely in sight when she was entertaining informally. Her daughters knew her ways and how much she enjoyed company. 'I'm so glad Mummy is coming to lunch', said one of them jokingly. 'But do be frightfully careful and not let her have a glass of port afterwards – she'll be here all afternoon'.

Scottish thrift, born in the First World War, never deserted the Queen Mother. When Princess Margaret was expecting her babies, her mother sent round her old, roomy shot-silk coats to be made into maternity dresses. They were later passed on to Lady Elizabeth Anson who said: 'They are very good about hand-me-downs'.

Always a realist, the Queen Mother – like Earl Mountbatten – planned her own funeral, even down to the candles for her Lying in State. 'I don't terribly like yours – may I provide my own', she requested. But until that sad day came, life continued to be an adventure – even in her nineties. She looked forward keenly to her birthday presents, especially if they were anything like the superb gifts she received on her eightieth birthday. A particular favourite was the inspiration of a group of close friends who clubbed together to give her a rather special fishing lodge on the Dee near Birkhall. Complete with dining-room and kitchen, it was the scene of many a happy informal luncheon party.

Among the many friends whose company she enjoyed were Dame Vera Lynn, who evoked so many wartime memories, Sir Woodrow Wyatt, who shared her interest in racing, and Lord and Lady Carrington. Although she missed those who had died, it would have been uncharacteristic for the Queen Mother to look backwards. 'It is always today and tomorrow', said another old friend, Sir Roy Strong. Her official duty diary was crammed with engagements for the next six months. Her personal dates with friends – racing, house parties in Scotland and at Royal Lodge – were all eagerly anticipated.

One of the Queen Mother's sayings, much quoted in the

family is: 'Work is the rent you pay for the room you occupy on earth'. It was her usual reply to gentle reminders that she no longer needed to work so hard. She said it with a mischievous smile, knowing her daughter had been brought up on this philosophy of the importance of duty. Then went serenely on with her arrangements.

The Queen Mother, like Princess Margaret, was a night bird and in the past rarely went early to bed. But, in her nineties, she retired earlier often with a book of poetry which she read until she fell asleep. Or a Dick Francis thriller chosen because he was her former steeplechase jockey and his plots are set in the world of horse-racing.

Her 'Guardian Angels' stood at each end of the four-poster bed. They were made of stone with carved haloes and wore robes which had to be washed and starched every few weeks. Like her sitting-room the bedroom was blue – that soft, hazy shade the Queen Mother loved and often chose for her clothes. Granddaughter-in-law Sarah, Duchess of York is often criticized for 'gilding the lily' in her choice of clothes. The Queen Mother had been doing it for years but nobody ever criticized her taste. 'Perhaps a few more pearls and tiny diamonds', she would suggest to the late Norman Hartnell, her courturier, if she thought an already well-festooned evening dress too bare. 'My sparklers', she called her jewellery, fabulous by even the Queen's standards, particularly the diamonds.

Her major illness, as a result of which she underwent a colostomy, was an uncomfortable period in her life, but overcome with typical courage. A subsequent painful leg ulcer, which still recurred, and a salmon bone which lodged in her throat – 'fought back' as she put it – were brushed aside as being 'so boring'.

'My little family', as she called the men and women of her staff, looked after their royal mistress carefully and tenderly. They would stay up until the early hours when she entertained and do anything to ensure her comfort and well-being. Her steward, William Tallon, remembers when he first met the Queen Mother during a 'Paul Jones' at a staff ball at Balmoral when he was just a lad. She asked him, as they danced, about his job. 'I wait on the senior staff, Your Majesty', he replied. 'Ah well . . . We all have to start somewhere', she said.

Racing remained a great interest. She called her horses 'My darling Boys' and had a bookie's blower installed at Clarence House so that she could follow events at any racecourse. On her desk each day was a copy of *The Sporting Life* which she scanned from cover to cover.

The Queen Mother never for a moment contemplated re-marriage after the King died in 1952. But she was always surrounded by a gallant band of men friends, most of whom were a little in love with her – just as they were when she was the young Duchess of York in the Twenties and early Thirties. She enjoyed clever, erudite conversation and particularly appreciated the quiet droll wit of friends like Lord Carrington and ex-premier Lord Home who, with their wives, were frequent guests.

In her homes, the Queen Mother liked things to be comfortable, cosy and even a little shabby. Carpets were well worn and chair covers often needed renewing, as they do in Buckingham Palace. One sofa leg was a favoured stopping place for one of her corgis who sometimes forgot the house rules. At Royal Lodge two armchairs needed recovering so badly her daughters clubbed together and presented their mother with new covers – 'Don't you think they are charming?' she asked guests.

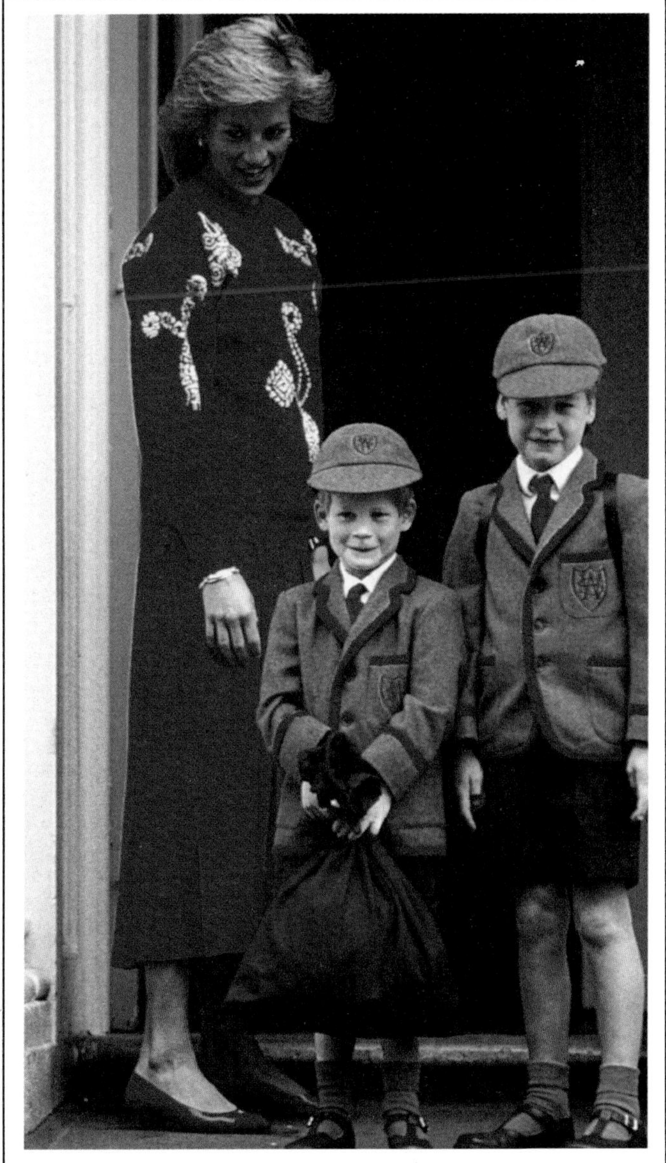

Princes William and Harry off to school.

All her life the Queen Mother had friends in every age group. She enjoyed the company of the 'arty' friends surrounding her granddaughter Lady Sarah Armstrong-Jones (now Chatto) who was a student at the Royal Academy School. Her brother David often popped in to tell her about his latest achievements. The Queen Mother was greatly interested in both his careers – furniture maker and restaurateur, particularly as her great-nephew, Patrick, Earl of Lichfield, was a partner in the restaurant business. Sarah's career fascinated her too. This granddaughter is a talented artist who became a professional painter. The Queen Mother had her own exquisite collection of paintings to which she added over the years, among them an impressive collection of modern work. Collective paintings and antiques, particularly anything that once belonged to the Bowes Lyon family, was one of her interests. A small shop in Thurso near the Castle of Mey was where she often found treasures and it had her royal warrant sign over the door.

Another war – even an isolated conflict – in her lifetime, meant that the dread of losing someone dear to her was again always at the back of her mind. In April 1982 Britain despatched a task force to the Falklands with Prince Andrew, aged twenty-two, among the helicopter pilots of 820 Sea King Squadron aboard HMS *Invincible*. The Queen Mother had seen so much anguish and heartache during two world wars. Now, like all the Royal Family, she lived through a private nightmare as she waited for news. The young Prince distinguished himself in the battle, especially when his helicopter was used as a decoy for the Exocet missiles.

Soon after the end of the war came the joyful news of a son for Charles and Diana – and another great-grandchild for the Queen Mother. Prince William was born on 21 June 1982, followed by Prince Harry on 15 September 1984.

As the year 2000 approached, the media preoccupation with anything or anybody 'royal' grew in intensity. The sense of balance the Queen Mother brought to royal publicity, with the judicious blend of distant monarch surrounded by an idyllic family, was in danger of developing into an unrealistic and glamorized peep show. Since the reign of George VI, interest in events such as royal weddings, jubilees, and even funerals, has mushroomed dramatically into a world-wide tableaux, courtesy of satellite television. Interest thus stimulated inevitably generated the media obsession with the Royal Family that so disturbed the Queen and other senior royals. 'How to keep the pot gently simmering but in no danger of boiling over is the question', said one close to the heart of this royal conundrum. The Queen Mother's policy, first developed in the Thirties, of preserving the royal 'mystique' at all costs, may well be the course to take, as her influence remained strong within the family circle, particularly with Prince Charles.

But how far the Queen Mother's wisdom and natural shrewdness would go in advising against any 'normalizing' of the Royal Family remains to be seen. Her aim, from the time she became Queen Consort and original master-mind of the House of Windsor's public image, had been to uphold the traditional virtues of family life – a concept in which divorce inside the Royal Family itself was not, at one time, tolerated. The fact that both Princess Margaret, Princess Anne and her brothers have suffered the anguish and failure of broken marriages was a great sadness to the Queen Mother, whose policy in life had always been, 'Grit your teeth and try harder'.

In the early years of the twentieth century the young Elizabeth Bowes Lyon was instilled with the virtues of determination and stoicism by her mother. This solid grounding during her most formative years might well have been the secret of her long and remarkable life.

In July 1988 the Queen Mother visited Wakefield Barracks to present colours and inspect a guard of honour.

OPPOSITE ABOVE: *The wedding of Prince Andrew and Sarah Ferguson – balcony scene at Buckingham Palace.*

OPPOSITE BELOW: *On Prince Andrew's wedding day his grandmother rode to Westminster Abbey with his aunt Princess Margaret and cousins Viscount Linley and Sarah Armstrong-Jones.*

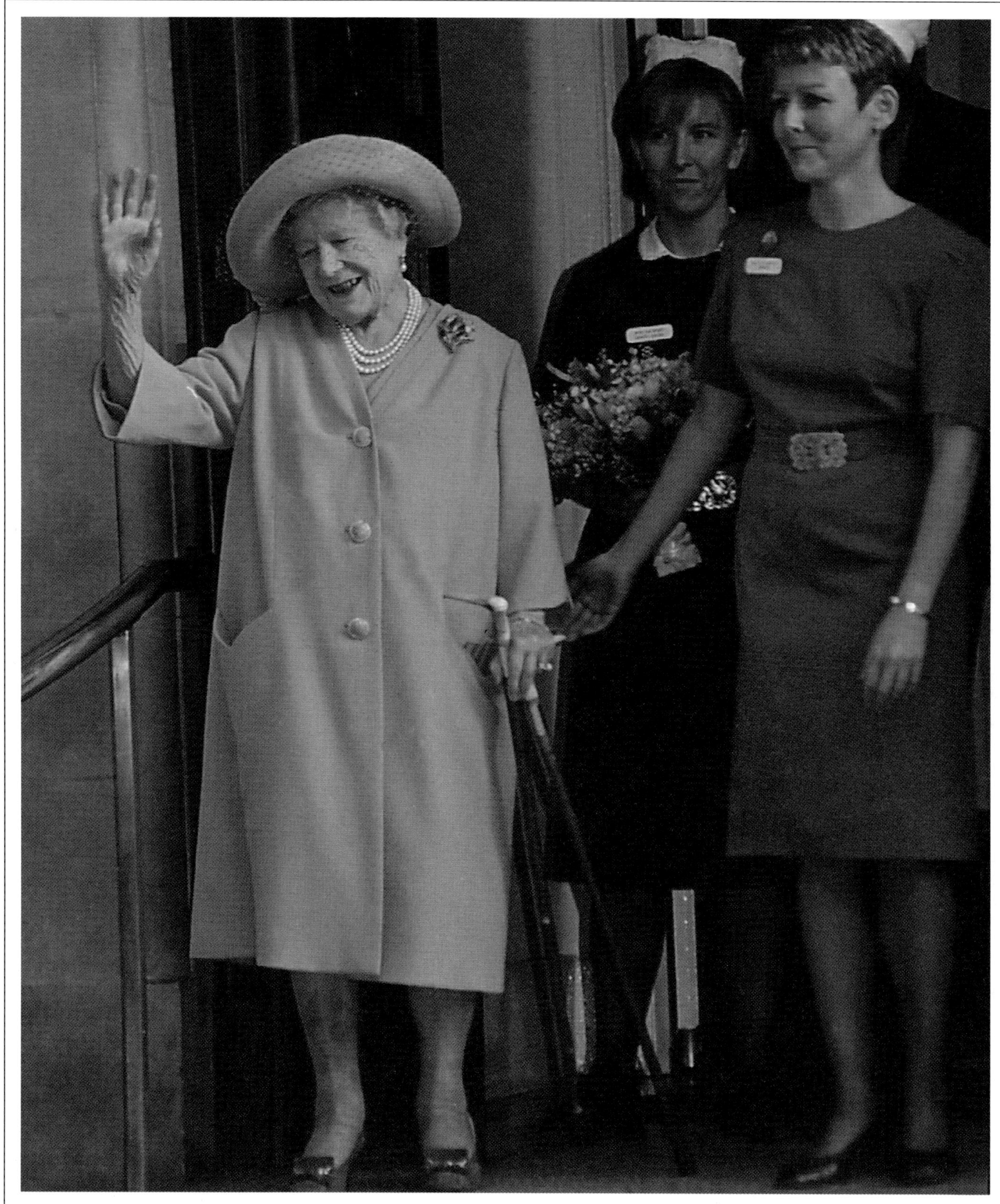

The Queen Mother leaves hospital after her second hip operation following a fall at Sandringham. Those close to her knew she was determined to return to public life as soon as possible to help a Royal Family in crisis after the death of Diana.

CHAPTER 10

ALL SHALL BE WELL

One of the Queen Mother's dearest friends once said of her: 'She loves her memories and we often look back over the marvellous years. But she feels yesterday is gone. It is today and tomorrow that are important'.

Sadly there are no more tomorrows for the woman who gave so much to the life of the century in Britain and the Commonwealth. At Clarence House, her London home, the bookie's 'blower' she had installed to hear the racing results, is silent. The telephone operator at Buckingham Palace does not ring through, as one has done since Elizabeth II's accession, first thing every morning to say: 'Your Majesty, Her Majesty is on the line'.

Most significantly of all the gilt and crystal triptych on her desk, the central panel holding the list of the day's engagements, is empty for the first time since Lawrence Whistler designed it as the gift of a former private secretary.

For, even in her nineties, as the century she had lived through ebbed and she was a very old lady, the Queen Mother continued to fulfil public duties. 'Work is the rent you pay for life', her mother had said in those faraway Edwardian days, and she had never forgotten.

After her second hip operation in January of 1998 she recuperated briefly and was back in public life by the late spring, helping to restore the Royal Family's vacillating fortunes with the familiar smile and the steadying presence.

Although she was never heard to voice them in public, in private she liked to ponder on a saying of the fourteenth century mystic Julian of Norwich: 'All shall be well'. Those comforting words had been embroidered on a golden banner which hung from a pillar opposite the altar at her eightieth birthday thanksgiving service at St Paul's. Afterwards the Queen Mother took it home with her and it was a constant reminder of the philosophy she lived by.

Years before, she had remembered those four small words during the Abdication crisis, the Second World War, the death of her beloved husband King George VI and, more recently, during the extended traumas that beset the Royal Family in the last years of her life.

As she fought the frailties of extreme old age with typical grit and fortitude, she sought to encourage her family, reeling from one disaster to another, that all would, in the end, be well. It had been a small, tightly knit unit. Then, in the nineties, there lay three marriages in ruins and a family the media were beginning to call 'dysfunctional'.

The supreme irony was that the Queen Mother, once an outsider herself, who married into the Royal Family, had welcomed the marriages of her grandchildren to partners from a world very different from 'the goldfish bowl' as the Duke of Edinburgh once described life behind palace walls.

It was his grandmother who ignored, or simply did not see, the danger signals and encouraged Prince Charles to marry Lady Diana Spencer, a young girl from a background very similar to her own: a demure Earl's daughter with no track record to mar the royal line. It was a misalliance now so obviously doomed that one wonders no one spotted the contrasting personalities that were to splinter and finally rupture that ideal family the Queen Mother had so lovingly fashioned all those years ago. Divorce, the hated D-word she so abhorred and had been so inflexible about during her reign as Consort, became the last resort in the marriages of three of her grandchildren.

First, Princess Anne, the Princess Royal, who handled it with a dignity that earned much respect, and has since remarried happily. Then came the saga of the Duke and Duchess of York who ruined Christmas in 1991 by telling the Queen of their marriage problems.

When she discussed this crisis with her mother neither of them knew that another far greater and more significant drama was unfolding. A few months later, in 1992, forty years after the Queen's accession and the Queen Mother's widowhood, a small, slim book was published that became the catalyst for the most serious threat to the future of the monarchy since the Abdication.

Andrew Morton's biography of Diana had been inspired

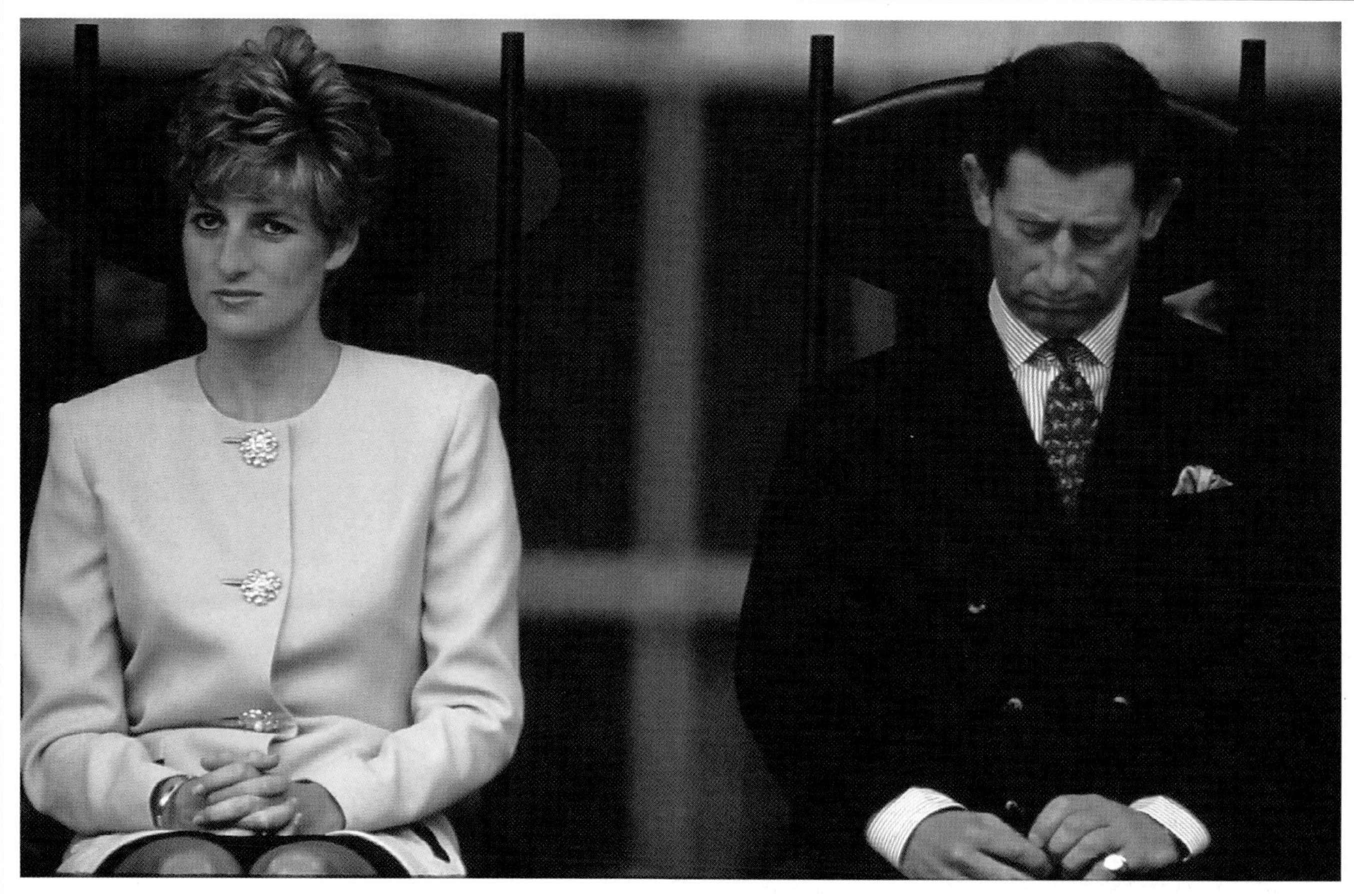

Now it was all too obvious their marriage was doomed. But it was a great sadness for the Queen Mother when the separation of the Prince and Princess of Wales was announced in 1994 and their divorce in 1996.

by the Princess herself and written largely with the help of tapes she used to tell her story to Morton. The Royal Family did not know it at the time although it was said that Charles himself felt that the material could only have come from his wife.

There followed an uneasy summer with open hostility between Charles and Diana. The Queen Mother, ever loyal to her beloved Charles, still did not deviate from her policy of rarely showing her true feelings. She maintained an outer calm, although she is said to have expressed herself forcibly to her daughter, the Queen, on the subject of love and loyalty.

Diana herself said of the Queen Mother: 'His grandmother is always looking at me with a strange look in her eyes. It's not hatred. It is sort of interest and pity mixed into one. I don't understand it. Every time I look up, she's looking at me and then looks away and smiles'.

In August 1992, when they were all at Balmoral, compromising pictures of the Duchess of York with a Texan lover, John Bryant, appeared in a tabloid newspaper. Four days later another tabloid published the 'Squidgygate' tapes, so called because 'Squidgy' was apparently the Princess's nickname and appeared throughout the recording of a telephone conversation between Diana and her friend James Gilbey. In it her feelings about the Royal Family were laid bare. In fact, the conversation had to be censored by the newspaper because of the language used and the implications it contained.

The Queen Mother, who normally adopted an 'ostrich' attitude to anything unpleasant, was profoundly shocked but nevertheless agreed with the Queen that no effort should be spared to try and salvage the marriage. But this time her usual advice to 'grit your teeth and try harder' did not have the desired results. Both the Prince and Princess had exhausted their attempts for a reconciliation and in 1994 agreed to separate.

That same year, on 20 November, the Queen's forty-fifth wedding anniversary, saw Windsor Castle ablaze, something the Nazis had never achieved throughout the wartime blitz. The Royal Family were, in Prince Andrew's words, 'absolutely devastated'. It had initially been a small fire, started by a restorer's lamp, but it spread rapidly. At its height

The Duchess of York's affair with American John Bryant was starkly revealed to the Royal Family by compromising pictures which appeared in a tabloid newspaper when they were all on holiday at Balmoral.

flames lit up the ancient castle and could be seen for miles around. Fortunately Prince Andrew, trained in disaster situations in the Navy, was in the castle. He speedily organized chains of helpers to carry out furniture and paintings and, as a result, very little was lost. But to the Queen Mother watching helplessly as television showed the castle ramparts devoured by flames and the Queen, in raincoat and headscarf, already at the scene, it was as if an era was coming to an end. All the Royal Family felt there might be something symbolic about the Windsor fire. The beginning of the end, perhaps, of their dynasty's 1,000-year-old reign?

But, resilient as its present occupiers, the historic castle rose again, not without controversy. When Peter Brooke, then Secretary of State for National Heritage, announced that public money would pay for the restoration there was an outcry. As a result the Queen decided to open Buckingham Palace to the public which eventually paid seventy-five per cent of the bill. It had been, as she said in a Guildhall speech four days later, her 'annus horribilis'. Combined with the antics of some of the younger members of the family, it was a nightmare period for the Queen and the Queen Mother and, again, the reason behind the criticism undoubtedly had its roots in the failure of the royal marriages and the behaviour of those concerned. A Gallup poll underlined this when it found that 'too many members of the Royal Family lead an idle, jet-set kind of existence'. It was a charge that could never have been levelled at the Queen Mother and she could have been forgiven for feeling that, perhaps, she had lived just a little too long to adapt comfortably to the changes she had to accept in her family circle.

Significantly, it was at about this time that she gave Princess Margaret permission to begin to destroy the most personal of her private papers. Never very methodical, the Queen Mother tended to leave private and personal correspondence lying around in her sitting room. Discreet to the end she did not wish her innermost feelings about the last years of her life ever to become public or to be known to future generations of her family. But as Kenneth Morgan, a constitutional historian put it: 'It is regrettable and a shame they have been destroyed. The Queen Mother has had such

In 1994, during the Queen's 'annus horribilis' and on her forty-fifth wedding anniversary, a great fire raged at Windsor Castle. 'The Nazis did not achieve that during the blitz' the Queen Mother observed, 'although we always feared they might'.

an extraordinary and long life and we need all the public material we can get. If you don't have it myths accumulate.' He added: 'In recent years the monarchy has been through extraordinary trials and tribulations. She has seen it all and done it all. Even if she has not been involved with policy-making, she has been around those who have made the decisions'.

Letter-writing was always a great pleasure to the Queen Mother and it became even more so as she grew older and was less active. Her great-niece Lady Elizabeth Anson told me that her collection of letters from the Queen Mother, written on her distinctive dove-grey paper with a black E R cypher, were among her most cherished possessions. Another relative described her 'beautiful writing and delicious turn of phrase'.

It was a great sadness for the Queen Mother when the separation between the Prince and Princess of Wales was announced in 1994. She said how glad she was that her great friend and lady-in-waiting, Lady Ruth Fermoy, grandmother of the Princess, who died in 1993, had been spared the decision.

A few weeks later came more distress for the two Elizabeths. Another taped conversation was sold to a tabloid newspaper. This time it was between Charles and Camilla Parker Bowles and was inevitably dubbed 'Camillagate'. In it the sexual content was explicit and shocked both the Royal Family and Middle England.

In December 1993, Diana made her dramatic 'withdrawing from public life' statement. Later in the month the Queen Mother, undoubtedly feeling shattered by recent events but still as outwardly calm as ever, slipped off to Scotland for Princess Anne's second wedding to former royal equerry Commander Tim Laurence. The deliberately quiet wedding must have brought back some memories of her younger daughter who threw away the chance of happiness with another royal equerry, Group Captain Peter Townsend, because of her 'duty' to the crown and pressure from the Establishment.

The next stage in the tragic royal soap saga was when the Princess of Wales's affair with her lover James Hewitt was revealed in a book called *Princess in Love*. In 1995 in her 'Panorama' interview Diana confirmed that she had indeed

The bond between the Queen Mother and her younger daughter, Princess Margaret, was always close. It was to 'Margot' that her mother turned when she felt certain of her most personal and private papers should be destroyed. Always discreet, she clearly did not wish her innermost feelings aired for posterity.

been in love with Hewitt. 'I adored him,' she said. Her interview was thought to be in retaliation for Prince Charles's television talk with Jonathan Dimbleby in June 1994. The Queen Mother who loyally supported him was nevertheless sure it was a mistake. She felt a dignified silence would have been more appropriate. That year he stayed with his grandmother at Birkhall, appearing at Balmoral only briefly for the 'ghillies' ball'.

He was said to have hurt his mother by appearing to blame the failure of his marriage on his parents and the lack of demonstrable affection that Charles felt he had missed as a child. It was not only the Queen Mother, who had pioneered the art of making a palace a home, who felt for her daughter. Her other three children appeared to disagree with Charles. Princess Anne is on record as saying: 'The greatest advantage of my entire life is the family I grew up in. I'm eternally grateful for being able to grow up in the sort of atmosphere that was given to me and to have it continue now that I'm grown up'.

When Diana said on 'Panorama' that she wanted to reign as the 'Queen of people's hearts', the Queen Mother saw yet another twist in what was becoming a tale entwined with irony. In the worst days of the Second World War, she and her husband King George VI had been affectionately known as 'the King and Queen of People's Hearts' because of their insistence on staying in the front line during the blitz on London and their indestructable loyalty to the nation and each other.

The 'Panorama' interview saw the last stages of the 'War of the Waleses'. It was becoming too dangerous to the monarchy to let it continue. Before Christmas 1995, after consultation with advisers, including her husband and mother, the Queen told the couple that divorce seemed the only option.

After her decree nisi which was granted on 15 July 1995, Diana, single once again, became an international woman of stature, a power player on the world stage culminating in her worldwide anti land-mines campaign.

If 1994 had been an 'annus horribilis', 1997 was even worse. The pressure was stepped up for fundamental royal reforms and a radical streamlining of the Royal Family. And on the last day of August, in a Paris road tunnel,

In 1995 in her 'Panorama' interview Diana confirmed she had an affair with James Hewitt.

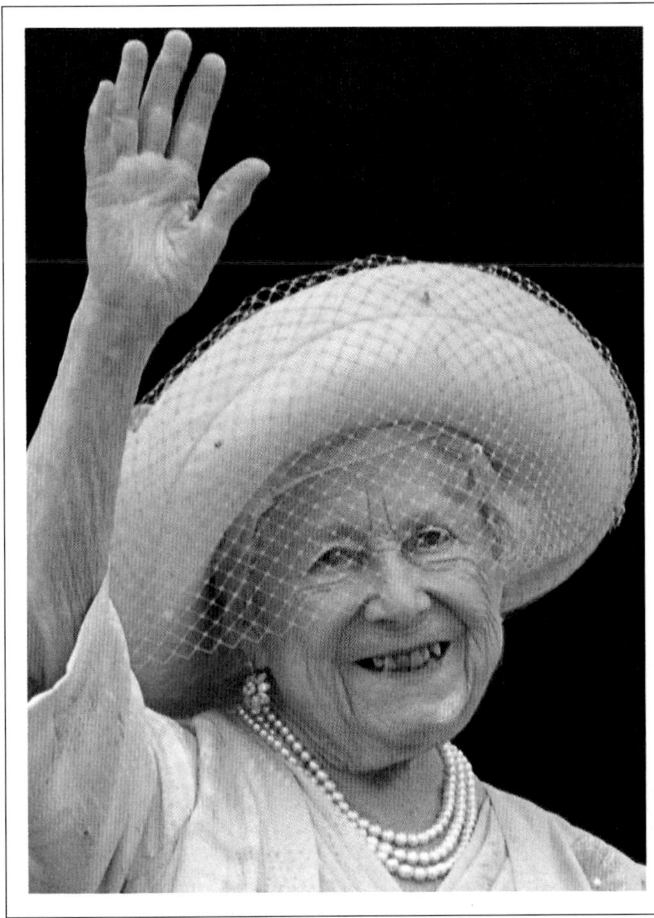

are not supposed to be human'. But at the end of the century they were expected to be not only human but 'touchy-feely' human like the now legendary Diana.

As public opinion swung for and against the royals, only the Queen Mother's popularity remained steady. When she fell over while visiting the racing stables at Sandringham early in 1998 and needed another hip replacement, the hospital and Clarence House were showered with flowers, letters and cards from all over the world. And in 2000 the celebrations to mark her 100th birthday drew thousands of well-wishers to the streets of London.

It was not in her nature to be over-demonstrative. But, like Diana, she had the common touch and a warmth that made people love her all her life. She once said of herself: 'I must admit that at times I felt something flow out of me. It makes me very tired for a moment. Then I seem to get something back from people – sympathy, goodwill. I do not know exactly but I feel strength again, in fact, recharged. It is an exchange I expect'. An exchange so unique and rewarding that even the changes wrought by the passage of time never diminished it.

4 August 2000: the Queen Mother acknowledges the cheers of the crowd outside Buckingham Palace on her 100th birthday.

Diana Princess of Wales was killed in a horrific car crash along with her friend Dodi Fayed. The Royal Family, on holiday at Balmoral, awakened that morning not only to darkest tragedy but to the realization that the woman who had been stripped of her HRH title was fast becoming a martyr in the most extraordinary worldwide scenes of grief.

Everything the Queen and her immediate family did aroused criticism and a feeling of censure that they had not supported the Princess when she needed them. Even the decision to stay at Balmoral for a few days as the family gave what comfort they could to Princes William and Harry was misunderstood. Public resentment deepened by the day. Only the Queen's television appearance eased the situation.

Three months after Diana's death, the Queen spoke more frankly than usual about the problems of being royal. 'The message is often harder to read, obscured as it can be by deference, rhetoric of the conflicting currents of public opinion. But read it we must'.

Half a century ago the Queen Mother observed with an edge of bitterness unusual in her: 'We, the Royal Family,

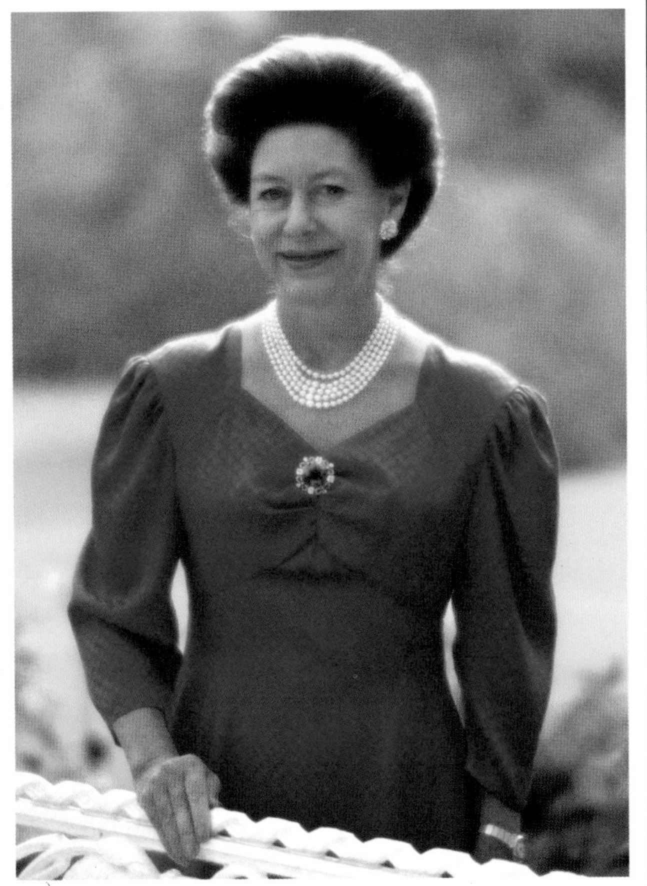

Princess Margaret died on 9 February 2002 after a series of strokes, having suffered several years of ill-health. Although frail, the Queen Mother attended her funeral at Windsor Castle

Her Majesty Queen Elizabeth The Queen Mother
died peacefully in her sleep at the age of 101 on 30 March 2002

Elizabeth R

ACKNOWLEDGEMENTS

AMONG friends and relatives who – on or off the record – helped in research and gave me a glimpse of the family woman behind the façade of majesty, I should particularly like to thank Lady Elizabeth Anson, the Queen Mother's great-niece, granddaughter of her elder brother John and god-daughter of King George VI. While maintaining the usual discretion of all those close to royalty, she still managed to convey the warmth, love and sheer joy of living so appreciated by those who really knew Queen Elizabeth, the Queen Mother – and the many who feel they did.

I am indebted, also, to the work of the late Lady Cynthia Asquith, friend and biographer of the Queen Mother whose invaluable first-hand reminiscences are quoted in the early chapters of this book.

PICTURE CREDITS

COLOUR

Camera Press Anthony Crickmay Frontispiece, 118, 125 (above)

Tim Graham 120

Her Majesty the Queen, reproduced by gracious permission 26, 28

Photographers International half title, 5 (above, centre, below), 7, 9, 13, 49, 50, 51, 52 (above, below left, below right), 53, 54, 55, 56, 105, 106, 107, 109, 114 (above, below), 115, 116 (above), 117, 125 (below), 126

Rex Features 121, 122, 123

Topham Picture Library 11, 12 (above), 16, 31, 32, 34, 37, 46, 82, 83, 108, 116 (below)

BLACK AND WHITE

Camera Press 101

Hulton Picture Company 75, 79 (below), 81, 84 (right), 85, 88, 98 (left, right), 104 (above)

Photographers International 67 (below), 101

Popperfoto 19, 22, 73, 84 (left), 90 (above), 91 (below), 92 (right), 100 (above), 102, 111

Rex Features 124

Syndication International 10 (left), 15, 17, 18, 21, 23, 27, 28, 33, 41, 44, 47, 63 (below), 104 (below)

Topham Picture Library 8, 10 (right), 12 (below), 14, 20, 25, 29, 36 (left, right), 39, 40, 42, 45, 48, 58, 59, 60, 61, 62 (above left, above right, below), 63 (above), 64, 65, 66, 67 (above), 68, 69, 70, 72, 74, 76 (above, below), 77, 78 (above, below), 79 (above), 80, 86, 87, 89, 90 (below), 91 (above), 92 (left), 93, 94, 95, 96, 97, 99, 100 (below), 110, 113

BIBLIOGRAPHY

Thatched with Gold: Mabell, Countess of Airlie. Hutchinson, 1962

Duchess of York: Lady Cynthia Asquith. Hutchinson, 1935

The King and his Country: Aubrey Buxton. Longmans Green & Co, 1955

The Strenuous Years/The Parting Years: Cecil Beaton. Weidenfeld & Nicolson, 1978

Diaries of Sir Henry Channon: Edited by Robert Rhodes James. Weidenfeld & Nicolson, 1967

The Little Princesses: Marion Crawford. Cassell, 1950

Edith Sitwell: A Unicorn Among Lions: Victoria Glendinning. Oxford University Press, 1983

Silver and Gold: Norman Hartnell. Evans Bros Ltd, 1955

King George VI: Denis Judd. Michael Joseph, 1982

The Queen Mother: Elizabeth Longford. Weidenfeld & Nicolson, 1981

Queen Elizabeth, the Queen Mother: Patrick Montague Smith. Hamlyn, 1985

Queen Elizabeth: Penelope Mortimer. Viking, 1986

Diaries and Letters: Harold Nicolson. Weidenfeld & Nicolson, 1967

King George VI and Queen Elizabeth: Christopher Warwick. Sidgwick & Jackson, 1985

Diana Cooper: Philip Ziegler. Hamish Hamilton, 1981

INDEX

Page numbers in *italics* denote illustrations.

People are indexed according to their married name, their present title or the title they had at their death.